CONCILIUM

concilium 1996/1

FEMINIST THEOLOGY IN DIFFERENT CONTEXTS

Edited by

Elisabeth Schüssler Fiorenza and M. Shawn Copeland

SCM Press · London
Orbis Books . Maryknoll

Published by SCM Press Ltd, 9–17 St Albans Place, London N1
and by Orbis Books, Maryknoll, NY 10545

ISBN: 0 334 03036 6 (UK)
ISBN: 0 88344 888 2 (USA)

Typeset at The Spartan Press Ltd, Lymington, Hants
Printed by Mackays of Chatham, Kent

Concilium Published February, April, June, August, October, December.

Contents

Feminist Theologies in Different Contexts

Introduction

In the last decade many different feminist theological voices have emerged around the globe so that it is no longer appropriate to speak of feminist theology in the singular. Conceptualizing feminist theologians in the plural allows one to glimpse the richly coloured tapestry of feminist theological thought and religious struggles world-wide. Therefore, it seems right to pause here for reflecting on the past ten years of feminist theology in *Concilium*. This issue seeks to celebrate not only feminist theological struggles and intellectual achievements during the past decade but also to chart future directions of feminist theology in various cultural and religious contexts. For that reason, this issue of *Concilium* aims to create a rhetorical space or an 'imaginary round-table' for the discussion of feminist theology in its manifold forms and articulations.

We invite readers to participate in this imaginary round-table in which different feminist theological voices partake, discuss and assess crucial theological matters, theoretical tensions and practical conflicts. We understand such differences and tensions not as fixed positions but as creative possibilities for solidarity and dialogue. In a context of increasing 'fundamentalist-nationalist' backlash against women, especially those marginalized and oppressed, as well as against feminist religious and political movements, the authors seek to communicate to a wider public the rich theological argument and possibility introduced by feminist theologies. They provide not simply descriptive accounts but also critical analyses of the articulations and struggles of feminist theologies in different geographical contexts and particular religious situations. Those articles analyse not only distinctive cultural but also diverse theological-religious frames of meaning and articulate particular global social locations. We hope that this theological 'round-table' indicates the rich theoretical and practical possibilities for feminist theologies in the 1990s and energizes readers not only to continue the conversation but also to practice 'difference in solidarity' in their own contexts of struggle.

In light of the religious and socio-political global contexts of our theologizing it is also appropriate to explore critically the social-institutional location of feminist theology in *Concilium*. The first issue of Feminist Theology in *Concilium* appeared ten years ago (1985). During the last decade *Concilium* has brought to the global development of feminist theology its own specific theological voice and approach. From its very conception feminist theology in *Concilium* had to struggle not only for its legitimacy, integrity and independence but also for its own theological voice. Despite pressures to the contrary, feminist theology in *Concilium* has not been conceptualized either as addressing the 'women in the church' question, or as theology by women for women, or, more fashionable, as 'gender theology'. Rather, it has been articulated and elaborated as a critical feminist theology of liberation in different theological accounts and diverse cultural-religious languages. As such it has not been conceptualized along traditional theological disciplinary lines which would begin the discussion of a theological theme with Scripture, go to dogma, and end with practical application.

The diverse *Concilium* issues of Feminist Theology have sought to embody and pioneer the approach of a critical feminist theology of liberation which begins with the systemically reflected experience of women and hence expresses different perspectives and social-religious locations. Consequently, all individual issues which have appeared until now have focused on the diverse forms and crucial areas of women's oppression and diverse struggles for liberation. They have theologically explored topics such as *Women – Invisible in Church and Theology, Women, Work and Poverty, Motherhood: Experience, Institution, Theology, A Special Nature of Women?, Violence Against Women*, from different social locations and feminist liberationist perspectives. Thereby they have sought to anchor feminist theological analyses and spiritual visions in diverse women's experiences of dehumanization and survival rather than measure and evaluate them with traditional theological criteria and standards. Instead of gauging feminist experience and theological reflection in terms of malestream theology, they have sought to challenge and transform traditional theology in such a way that the experience of multiply oppressed women can move into the centre of theological reflection. Such a critical theological approach has resulted in an interdisciplinary ecumenical, interreligious and intercultural method that transgresses the traditional disciplinary boundaries of academic or ecclesiastical theology.

We are proud that the various *Concilium* issues of Feminist Theology have pioneered a different, 'new way' of doing theology and want to thank the members of the advisory board of Feminist Theology for their work and support. Although the existence and integrity of Feminist Theology in *Concilium* is far from being assured, we hope that we will be able to safeguard this unique forum of diverse feminist theologies in the years to come so that readers will be able to continue to hear these 'new' theological voices in their various global and spiritual inflections.

Elisabeth Schüssler Fiorenza

I · Different Geographical Sites of Struggle

Women's Voices in Latin-American Theology*

Maria José F. Rosado Nunes

'The first time I said, "You're wrong" to a great theologian friend of mine, I was shocked at myself; I thought it couldn't be me talking. It was not the first time I had thought differently from him on some aspects of theology, but I had never dared to express my disagreement. I had taken a leap forward in life . . . I had moved from being an echo to being a voice.'
(Elsa Tamez, *Las mujeres toman la palabra*, 1989)

Introducing the subject

Feminine courage has been very quiet on our continent, in the ecclesial sphere and even more so in that formerly absolutely forbidden to women: theology. In the seventeenth century, from 12 November 1651 to 17 April 1695, a most extraordinary woman lived in Mexico: Sor Juana Inés de la Cruz, whom Beatriz Melano Couch has called 'the first woman theologian in the Americas, North or South' (Couch, 1985, 51, 54).

Despite the three centuries that have elapsed since her death, one element in her life story has become contemporary, or sadly 'modern', as Octavio Paz says. At the end of her life, Sor Juana was forced to abandon her intellectual work, to get rid of her library and to spend her nights in 'penance and disciplines'. The 'conversion' imposed on her by the Holy Office was in fact her humiliation and confession of defeat. This was the upshot of the daring of this seventeenth-century woman, who defended women's, and particularly religious', right of access to full knowledge. How can we not recall the 'invitation' to study and the 'silence' imposed on Sister Ivone Gebara, on the eve of the twenty-first century, when reading Octavio Paz's words on Sor Juana: 'Her fate as a writer castigated by prelates sure of the truth of their opinions reminds us, men of the twentieth century, of the destiny of free intellectuals in societies dominated by orthodoxy and ruled by bureaucracy' (Paz, 1982, 629). This is also the moment to recall the cases of Leonardo Boff in Brazil, Uta Ranke-Heinemann in Germany, and so many women prevented in our time from teaching in theology schools or from attending courses reserved for the clergy, whose names we do not even know.

Women's voices in Latin-American theology

The 1960s to 1980s saw a great mobilization of women in Latin America. In the struggle for civil rights, faced with a situation of growing poverty under dictatorial military regimes, in urban and rural popular social movements, the women of the continent stood out for their intense participation in politics. In the religious sphere, in the Catholic and some Protestant churches, the period was marked by the formation and spread of base church communities (CEBs) and of the discourse that legitimized them, liberation theology. Large numbers of Catholic women were involved in the project for forming a 'church of the poor'.

It was in this socio-ecclesial context that women in Latin America started producing theology. The same process that mobilized Catholic women – lay women of the popular classes and religious – to form base communities, eventually also integrated some women in the process of working out theology. This access to theology came about, though, only in the 1980s, being therefore later than women's involvement in the base communities and the rise of liberation theology, which began to find its voice in the 1960s and 1970s.

Women theologians' first publications appeared in specialist pastoral reviews or in collective works of liberation theology. These formed the sphere of reference for women's theological thinking. From 1979 on, various meetings and seminars were organized on a continent-wide scale, bringing women from the Christian churches together. The first of these was held in Mexico, in a place particularly significant for women: close to Tepeyac. There, on the sacred mountain Tonantzin, the Goddess-Mother consoled the Aztec people oppressed by the white European invaders (Nauta and Goldewijk, 1987, 8ff.).

In the final document produced by this meeting, after assessing the base communities and liberation theology, the participants accentuated the situation of oppression in which women lived in the churches and in society as a whole. They noted the absence of 'a specific contribution from a women's viewpoint' in theological work, and urged the active participation of Latin American women, as intellectual agents within the popular process. Various other meetings followed: in San José in 1981, Managua in 1983, Bogotá in 1984, Buenos Aires in 1985, Oaxtepec in 1986. These meetings brought together women from different Christian confessions, encouraged and supported by international ecumenical bodies, such as EATWOT (Ecumenical Association of Third-World Theologians).

The theology produced by women in Latin America, and more specifically in Brazil, has its own special characteristics, stemming from the social and religious context in which it is worked out. It is, first, work that reflects the hegemonic position in the Catholicism of the period, of sectors engaged in discourse and pastoral practice aimed at 'those excluded from society', generically termed 'the poor'. Women theologians did not evolve their own methodology; following liberation theology, they started from the option for the poor and engagement in a praxis of liberation. If, however, women originally appeared – or disappeared – among the generality of the 'people', the discourse of women theologians gradually came to tackle the specificity of the situation of poor women. Several of their texts indicated women's poverty as the material for the act of 'doing theology'. They speak of the option for the poor as 'option for poor women'. In a surprising innovation, on becoming agents of the process of doing theology, they take as the object of their theological activity the situation of those who are excluded among the excluded: the women of the poor classes. Their work thus differs from that of male theologians, who deal with 'the poor' without reference to the distinctions that the fact of being men or women – as that of race – imposes on the way poverty affects these social categories and the way they experience poverty.

Besides this characteristic of engagement with the daily experience of women 'of the people', there is a second distinguishing feature of women's theology, at least in Brazil: the creation of ample opportunities for women theologians to meet and discuss among themselves. In 1985, the first national reunion was held on the subject of 'women's theological work in the Christian churches'. Several others followed. Christian women, theologians, pastors and pastoral agents in the base communities meet regularly to discuss relevant aspects of faith 'from the women's angle'. Besides this, gains are being made in the institutional sphere, with study groups and other bodies multiplying in theological colleges and universities. A 'feminist chair' has been instituted in IMES (the Methodist Institute of Higher Education) in Sao Bernardo do Campo, as a result of representations made by an organized group of women theologians. The formation of such groups is part of women's struggle for recognition of their right of full access to all areas of learning and intellectual speculation.

This is an important political advance, by no means confined to theology. Over the whole country, innumerable centres for feminist studies have been established over the past few years.

A third characteristic of women's studies in the theological field is their development in the area of biblical studies. Countless publications on 'women of the Bible' seek to rescue the outstanding female figures in the 'history of salvation', showing how important their presence and actions were in the development of the 'people of God'. Biblical studies, though, are not limited to this recovery of outstanding female personages; they rather concentrate on a broad reinterpretation of the whole of the sacred books in a sense favourable to women, revealing them as protagonists, in the full sense, in 'saving action'.

A feminist theology?

Classifying the theology produced by women in Latin America as 'feminist' raises a number of questions.[1] Some women theologians themselves find this nomenclature debatable. Taking a stance very close to that of 'leftist' tendencies, they regard feminism as a 'bourgeois and First-World' movement, so questioning its applicability to our situation. Or they see women's movements in our part of the world as so specific to the situation of the Third World that 'feminist' is an inadequate designation. This discussion is not confined to the feminist movement, as such, in Latin America. There are groups that identify themselves as definitely 'feminist', while others call themselves 'women's movements'.

Nevertheless, among women theologians closest to the feminist groups, this discussion is posited in a different form, and they speak of the need to develop their own theological discourse, one that addresses the questions raised by the feminist movement more directly. Gathered at the Fourth Feminist Conference of Latin America and the Caribbean, in 1987, these women, most of them active in base communities and women's organizations, took part in a workshop on 'Feminism and the Churches'. The final document they produced includes an analysis of the patriarchy operative in church institutions of the region and a proposal for ways ahead, to be worked out by women themselves, in terms of theology and worship. They said: 'We need to overcome the fear of developing our own theology; we need to interpret and systematize our own experiences in our Christian communities' (Nauta, 1987, 12). They then stress the positive contributions made by the churches of Latin America in the field of human rights and struggles for social justice, and the significance of liberation theology in overcoming situations of injustice and affirming 'the power of the poor to transform society'. Therefore, they add, 'we protest against the fact that liberation theology has not dealt with the specific oppression of women to a significant extent; for this reason, we consider urgent the development of a feminist liberation theology'.

The US theologian Beverley Harrison also stresses this ambivalence in liberation theology. After affirming the solidarity of feminists with liberation theologians, for whom theology is a reflection on praxis, she declares: 'But we must also say to the Latin Americans that every time you sniff power, whether in ecclesiastical hierarchies or theological associations, and every time you express what you have to say in relation to that power, women are invisible in the way you speak . . . ' (in Biehl, 1987, 92–3). The Peruvian theologian Rosa Trapasso follows the same critical line: 'It seems to me that liberation theology does not go far enough in questioning the basic roots of oppression or deep enough in studying the links between different forms of oppression, in a society such as that of Peru.' And she points to the reasons for this failing: 'Since liberation theology is generally run by male theologians, it does not question the prevailing *machismo* in the structures of society, which limits its capacity for contributing effectively to changing it . . . this model can be broken only by a will to examine the sin of sexism in the Church and a critique of the patriarchal structures that lie at the root of oppression in society' (in Nauta and Goldewijk, 1987, 6 n. 7). It is not without significance that this theologian's words were relegated to a footnote in the book in which they appeared, and that she was presented as a dissonant voice in the chorus of Latin American women theologians, many of whom 'do not wish to set themselves up in opposition to men theologians or their discourse' (*id.*, 4). A Brazilian woman theologian also affirms, without referring directly to liberation theology, that: 'Women theologians (in Latin America) mostly work on material produced by men and furthermore do not dare to criticize this material from a feminine standpoint, so as not to lose the ground they have won' (Gebara, 1989, 920).

So the different postures adopted by women theologians in Latin America show, on the one hand, their strong links with liberation theology and, on the other, the problems raised by this linkage. On the methodological level, what allowed 'women's experience' to become part of theological discourse was the breakthrough achieved by liberation theology, tying theological reflection to the experience of faith communities rather than to dogmatic discourse. 'We know that no one would pay attention to us, or hear what we are saying, if there had not been a large number of protests made by men theologians against the prevailing theological paradigms' (Harrison, in Biehl, 1987, 72).

The methodological evaluation of 'reality' undertaken by liberation theology made it possible for women theologians to use the concrete experiences of women as a 'hermeneutical key' for re-reading the Bible and religious traditions. Despite this, a problem arises when we try to define this 'women's experience'. 'In the mystique/policies put forward by progressive Latin American currents, women have still not broken through in their likeness and difference. The breakthrough of the poor has still not really viscerally integrated the breakthrough of women,' says Ivone Gebara. In utilizing Marxism as 'an instrument for analysing reality', liberation theology has not come to incorporate the critique made by socialist feminists – which can also be said, in general terms, of most theology produced by women in Latin America. This means that tackling problems related to the domination and exploitation of women in contemporary societies is often modelled, in many of these texts, on a reductionist class analysis. Social relationships are stratified, with sexual relationships, like those between races, being subordinated to class relationships.

This type of analysis produces political proposals – and pastoral practices – in which 'struggles' are classified as 'general' or 'specific' with one subordinated to the other. The latter are taken to include women's and race struggles. Overthrowing capitalism, as the existing political and economic system, is made the 'priority' task. 'Women are generally told that the process of social change requires priorities and strategies. And they then have to wait at the end of the line for their liberation. And in the end, as Ruether states, they have to disappear, serving other struggles than those specifically their own' (Biehl, 1987, 93).

In effect, establishing hierarchies in overcoming inequalities means postponing other emancipations, until 'basic needs' have been satisfied. And yet, defining what is understood as 'basic needs' and what is 'the main struggle' is a political task and should involve everyone, if an excluding definition is not to consolidate particular forms of oppression. In one centre for feminist studies, there was a humorous poster saying: 'If men got pregnant, abortion would be a "basic right".'

The words of two Latin American women theologians show the different positions held in the female theological milieu with regard to this question. One says: 'From this perspective, I can then identify fully with the struggle for life, with the struggle for a radical change aimed at affecting not sexual oppression but also, in the first place, class and racial oppression and exploitation' (in Tamez, 1986, 166). The other states: 'The change that comes through political and economic structures is very limited. Without confronting the problems of patriarchy and hierarchy –

which continue to oppress people on the basis of race, sex and class – there is little possibility of advance in the direction of a more just society' (in Nauta and Goldewijk, 1987, 16–17). While the first hierarchizes the oppressions suffered by the female population, the second stresses their links with other forms.

The difficulty some women theologians find in undertaking the discussions with Marxism referred to above is perhaps owing to the critical position adopted by men theologians with regard to feminism. 'It is because of Latin American theology', says one woman theologian, 'that I cannot impede the struggle of Latin American women by *misrepresenting* them on the lines of First-World feminism' (Tamez, 1986, 166: my italics). Just as in left-wing circles, so in Christian ones there is a value classification of the feminist movement. There is a 'bad feminism', for which there is no place in Latin America, 'against men'. This feminism informs a 'radical' theology, critical of the exclusion of women from positions of power in the church, preoccupied with problems such as the implications of the church's position on questions involving sexuality, reproduction or violence against women. Such questions are 'without interest' for women 'of the people', involved as they are in the daily struggle for survival, one way and another, gaining their 'voice' in the church through the base communities.

The 'good feminism', a gentle critic of ecclesial institutions, is the one that can be assimilated by traditional theology, as it can by liberation theology. This is because theology, by incorporating the 'women question', can keep women precisely as a 'topic'. 'Women' in a social or ecclesial setting come to be treated as chapter headings or the subject of 'specialized' books. In other words, the 'question' or 'subject of women' is incorporated only when it does not rock the already-established theological foundation, whether traditional or liberational. Men accept a certain openness and dialogue provided that the basic ways of looking at the world remain those 'that they themselves produce' (Gebara, 920). Recent books of theology – or of associated disciplines such as pastoral practice or catechesis – can deal with systematic theology or other subjects that seem to have nothing to do 'with women' by ignoring the 'subject' and producing a totally 'gender-neutral' (or 'race-neutral') discourse. Theology 'about women' is delegated to women, as if it were of interest only to this 'specific' group, while men continue to produce a supposedly 'universal' theology.

So, besides the 'economic reductionism' mentioned above, a certain 'biological essentialism' pervades a good part of Latin-American theological output. Constant references to the 'exceptional qualities' of women do nothing except confirm a supposed 'feminine nature'. Two Brazilian

women theologians, Nancy C. Pereira and Tânia V. Sampaio, comment-
ing on what liberation theologians say about women's theological work,
draw attention to this problem. According to them, classifying women's
theological work as closer 'to life' in its actuality and poetry, as opposed to
men's 'abstract' and 'rational' discourse, can actually reinforce the notion
that rational discourse is a male preserve – 'competent' discourse – while
'tender and affective' discourse is female. They ask: would not the type of
contribution made by women rather 'result from their condition as
oppressed and removed from more rational and abstract intellectual
development?' (in Tamez, 1989, 110–11).

One of the criticisms made by women social scientists of liberation
theology is precisely its reduction of socially constructed sexual categories
– gender – to biological characteristics. One of the indicators of this referral
of women to biology is their removal to 'feminine essence', to what is
'different', 'mysterious', to a sphere hovering beyond what is properly
'human', i.e. masculine, already explained by science and therefore
without 'mysteries'. One might ask here: what sort of social or market
acceptance would there be for a book titled 'The Masculine Secret of the
Mystery'? This enclosure of women under 'specific' headings comes up
against the feminist theologians' endeavour to deconstruct and reconstruct
theological discourse in its totality. 'We are not seeking simply to be
incorporated in androcentric theological or intellectual work,' says
Fiorenza, 'but have come to see the need to redefine and transform all
intellectual institutions and academic disciplines, if we want them to allow
women to participate as subjects and not as objects of university research
and theological science' (in Rosado Nunes, 1987, 27).

Feminist theologians deny the 'universal' pretension of existing
theology, pointing to its 'particular' character, i.e. the fact that it is made
from a male point of view and is therefore exclusivist. 'Recourse to the
experience of women thus explodes like a critical force, revealing classical
theology, including its named traditions, as being based on the experience
of men rather than on universal human experience' (Ruether, 1983, 13).
They propose a re-working that would allow the inclusion not only of
women, but also of non-whites, non-Westerners. Breaking patriarchal
structures requires, according to them, a radical change of 'paradigms'.
Børresen speaks of a 'real revolution affecting all human speech about God.
This would be the most profound paradigm-shift known in the history of
Christian doctrines', transforming not only 'human verbalizations on the
divine, but also the symbol system' (in Rosado Nunes, 1987, 27). It is not,
then, a matter of integrating women into a society and a church in which
the masculine still prevails as a norm, but of radically altering patriarchal

structures, which depend on a misogynist legitimation and an androcentric view of reality.

The problems of linking feminist theology with liberation theology appear again on anothr level: that of critique of church structures. The base communities and the 'Mothers' Clubs' linked to them are certainly contributing, to an extent unknown in the history of Catholicism, to ensuring the 'protagonism of poor women' within the church itself and within Brazilian society. The developments of this process, with the creation of autonomous groups of women within the base communities, or as breakaway groups from them, are thereby pointing up the limitations of church action in relation to the female population (Rosado Nunes, 1991). The inclusion of poor women in pastoral practice and ecclesial discourse is not, on its own, a guarantee of gain in terms of women's exercising autonomy in thought and action or of winning space within the institutional power structure. Socio-historical analysis of the process of integrating the female population on ecclesial projects shows, at least in the case of Brazilian Catholicism, that this tends more towards defending institutional interests in maintaining and even reinforcing the existing social and religious power structures than truly to taking women's concerns on board. It could not be any other way, given the absolutely masculine nature of religious power in the Catholic Church.

The constitutional dynamic of the so-called 'Church of the Poor' is no different. Recent inquiries reveal the lack of linkage between the base communities and the direct interests of women. 'I have never met or heard speak of a single Mothers' Club that had been formed with the intention of helping women to raise their own consciousness, or to act politically, as women,' says Sônia Alvarez. And she goes on: 'Besides this, the strategy of conscientization, so central to "mixed" groups such as the base communities, is rarely undertaken in Mothers' Clubs linked to the church, except in those formed on the initiative of the women themselves' (Alvarez, 1990, 23). Latin American theological discourse often exalts the 'participation' of women in the communities, without critically considering the ambivalence of this process. They are incorporated into a process that is not theirs, which they have not helped to plan, even if they can derive certain advantages from it.

Furthermore, the 'restorationist policies' (Benedetti, 1990) that have been gaining ground over the past few years in the Catholic Church, as evidenced from strict control of theological output to the 're-clericalization' of base groups – communities and parishes –, show the difficulties inherent in any attempt to invest lay people with real power in the Catholic Church. Now, any change in the status of lay people in the Catholic Church affects its female adherents in a radical manner, since all Catholic women, including religious, are excluded from access to the priesthood, are lay. And even 'more lay than lay men', since the internal laws that regulate the workings of the church – the Code of Canon Law – exclude them, explicitly, from functions which, in certain circumstances, are delegated to lay men in the community. 'Women are not, then, lay people, properly speaking, meaning people who enjoy the full rights of the baptized', writes Zimmermann (in Rosado Nunes, 1987, 30).

This means that any discourse that contains a proposal to include women effectively in Catholicism must necessarily subvert its present structures, by affecting the main pillar on which they rest, the clergy-lay distinction, with its attribution of sacred power to the former and the dispossession of the latter. A discourse that truly includes women presupposes a critique of the patriarchal structures of society – and of the church – and, therefore, presents itself as a discourse that deconstructs the power of men, in all social spheres, including the religious and symbolic. In this sense, it goes beyond the simple 'addition' of women to existing discourses and proposes the reformulation of the whole discourse. This is because there is no way of speaking of 'women' without immediately speaking of 'men', once they define one another as socially constructed categories. Now, liberation theology arose in the context of a church that was being innovative in the field of pastoral practice, politically confrontational against military dictatorship, in the case of Brazil, and allying itself, at least partially, with sectors of society working for radical change. At the same time, power within the Catholic Church institution shifted to the sector of the hierarchy that defended institutional innovations, on the level of discourse and practice, by proposing a degree of democratization of internal structures. So, in contrast to what happened in other Latin American countries, in Brazil the establishment of base communities and the elaboration of the theological discourse that legitimized and stimulated them were not carried out in opposition to the hierarchy. On the contrary, it was in agreement with the hierarchy that the 'Church of the Poor', or 'Christianity of Liberation', as it has been called (Lowy, M., 1988) was born. This does not, however, mean that there have not been some conflicts.

The strategy of working with the hierarchy, adopted by most radical groups and resulting from experience of earlier conflictive experiences that left a bad memory – such as the dismantling of Catholic Action in the 1960s –, is connected with the fact that most theologians are members of the clergy. Besides this, there are elements in the church history of the Catholic ecclesial institution in Brazil that explain this tendency to avoid rather than aggravate conflicts. Such a situation means that criticism of the patriarchal structures of the church is minimized, or at least set aside as inconvenient, because of internal institutional arrangements. It is not uncommon for existing conflicts with Rome to be invoked as justification for the impossibility of opening up a new flank in the battle by raising polemical issues relating to the 'question of women' in the church. For reasons that are not difficult to appreciate, the hierarchy reacts very strongly to any questioning of the ecclesial structure or the way it functions. Discourse revolving around the poor was partially assimilated by the institution and even incorporated into official discourse, though often in a sense differing markedly from that meant by liberation theologians, while theoretical and practical proposals for changes on the organizational level are found unacceptable. The condemnation of Leonardo Boff's *Church: Charism and Power*, and present difficulties with pastoral practices that invest lay men in the communities with symbolic and organizational power, are some indications of this state of affairs.

Finally, the theological output of Latin American women raises another question: that of its relationship to the feminist theology produced in the United States and Europe. This originated in the 1960s, closely linked to women's struggles in feminist movements and taking a critical stance in relation to the exclusion imposed on women inside the church institution. Mary Daly, with her *The Catholic and the Second Sex* (1968), can be considered its first representative in the Catholic camp. But in the 1950s, theological reflection had already been linked to the feminist movement in discussion on the ordination of women. This feminist theological writing was, however – and still is –, difficult to find in Latin America (Taborda, 1990, 312 n. 4). The Brazilian edition of *Concilium* introduced us to the thinking of several of these women, who published articles in the review. Elisabeth Schüssler Fiorenza's *In Memory of Her. A Feminist Theological Reconstruction of Christian Origins* was the first weighty work of feminist theology to be translated in Brazil, nearly ten years after its original appearance in English.[2] So this field of theological endeavour could become a point of reference for Latin American theology written by women only after considerable delay and to a somewhat restricted extent. Such a situation is indicative of the balance of power between women and men in the work sphere, in that of the dissemination of knowledge and inside institutions. Publishing houses here are run by men, and they did not consider US and European feminist theology worth translating, despite its volume, importance and the lively polemic aroused by its original-language publication. This theology was often discounted on grounds of its 'First World' character. Seen as remote from the concerns of

Latin American women, it was ignored as a reference point for theological work in the Third World.

In this way, male theologians became the main interlocutors for Latin American women theologians. They have till now been the champions of women's work, bestowing on them the legitimacy of their work as theologians. They have also been mainly responsible for women's appointments to academic posts, since, at least in Brazil, theological studies are confined to confessional universities, governed by clerics.

Even on the level of relations with Latin American feminism, there is a certain imbalance. Dialogue with feminists is recent, at any rate in Brazil. Opportunities for discussion between women theologians and women engaged in feminist work are only just beginning to be organized. This lack of contact stems from the histories of feminist struggles in the country as a whole and those of women within the Catholic Church, which have apparently run mostly on parallel lines, crossing only in conflictive situations. For Catholic women, the feminist camp was simply not 'their' camp. Still today, despite the vitality and originality of feminist movements on this continent, their claims and struggles have not yet been made the object of theological reflection, at least on the part of Christian women. Despite this, it seems that the last few years have seen a growing openness of women theologians to dialogue with feminists. On various occasions for theological-pastoral discussion – meetings, seminaries and the like – feminists are being invited to take part. This is also leading to a breaking down of barriers and prejudices held by feminists about women with a place in church institutions.

On the base level in the church, however, women of 'the people' are increasingly identifying with feminist discourse and practical proposals. The present situation – socio-political as well as ecclesial – encourages this coming together and recognition of common interests, even if differences are not entirely annulled. And it is perhaps precisely this movement of women on the fringes of society toward feminism that is awakening in women theologians suspicions of the possibilities such a coming together might offer in terms of the content and methods of a theology 'of women', or 'for women', or 'feminist' – and why not?

In conclusion

This article has dealt with the theological work undertaken by Christian women in Latin America, particularly in Brazil. It has not taken any particular study as a starting point, still less claimed to be an exhaustive examination of their work. My aim has been much more modest: I have sought to analyse the social and ecclesial conditions that have permitted the rise of this form of theological discourse in this part of the world, going on to outline some of its characteristics and the difficulties faced by women in producing it.

I should point out that reasons of lack of space and time have forced me to deal in the singular with both theology – feminist and liberation – and feminism, whereas both contain, as various analyses have shown, several currents. Without traducing this plural – or whatever one calls it – reality, I have tried here to establish connections and divergences, to state problems and to raise questions applicable, to a more or less general degree, to these different forms of discourse. As a Brazilian poet put it: 'I am not waiting for the day when all men [and women!] will agree: I just know of some pretty harmonies without a last judgment' (Caetano Veloso, *Fora da Ordem*).

Translated by Paul Burns

Notes

* A fuller version of this text was published in *Estudos Femistas*, no. O, CIEC/ECO/UFRJ, 1992 (Rio de Janeiro), under the title *De Mulheres e de Deuses*.

1. A recent thesis studies the theological production of women in Brazil: *Feminismo do sagrado – O dilema 'igualdade/diferença' na perspectiva de teólogas católicas* (Rio de Janeiro 1995).

2. See my criticism of the omission of the phrase 'In Memory of Her' from the title of the translation, in *Mulheres e Deuses*.

Bibliographical references

Alvarez, Sônia E., 1990., 'Women's Participation in the Brazilian "Peoples Church": A Critical Appraisal', in *Feminist Studies* 16, no. 2

Benedetti, Luiz Roberto, 1990, 'O impasse entre o politico e o religioso nas CEBs', in *Perspectiva Teologica* 58

Biehl, João Guilherme, 1987, *De Igual para Igual. Um Diálogo Crítico entre a Teologia de Libertaçao e as Teologias Negra, Feminista e Pacifista*. Petrópolis

Couch, Beatriz Melano, 1985, 'Sor Juana Inés de la Cruz. The First Woman Theologian in the Americas', in J. and E. Webster (eds.), *The Church and Women in the Third World*. Philadelphia, Pa.

Lowy, Michael, 1988, 'Marxisme et théologie de la libération', in *Cahiers d'Etude et de Recherche* 10

Nauta, Romic, 1987, 'Latin American Women's Theology', in *Exchange* 48

—— and Berma Klein Goldewijk, 1987, 'Feminist Perspectives in Latin American Liberation Theology', in *Exchange* 48

Paz, Octavio, 1982, *Sor Juana Inés de la Cruz o las Trampas de la Fe*, Barcelona

Rosado Nunes and Maria José Fontelas, 1987, 'Igreja Católica e Poder Feminino', in *Comunicaçoes do ISER* 27

———, 1991, *Eglise, sexe et pouvoir. Les femmes dans le catholicisme au Brésil – Le cas des communautés ecclésiales de base*, doctoral thesis, École des Hautes Études en Sciences Sociales, Paris

Ruether, Rosemary Radford, 1983, *Sexism and God-Talk, Toward a Feminist Theology*. Boston and London

Taborda, Francisco, 1990, 'Feminismo e teologia feminista no Primeiro Mundo. Breve panorâmica para uma primeira informaçao', in *Perspectiva Teologica*, 58

Tamez, Elsa, 1986, *Teólogos de la liberación hablan sobre la mujer*, San José, Costa Rica

———, 1989, 'Las mujeres toman la palabra', in *Diálogo con Teólogos de la liberación*. San José, Costa Rica

Weaving a Strong Web: Feminist Theo/alogizing in an Australian Context

Elaine Wainwright

'Feminist theology for women in Australia is not something one can find primarily in books. It occurs, rather, in the daily, urgent, sometimes desperate exploration, reassessment and recreation of meaning which women are continually making in their lives. In this sense, feminist theology is the collective and individual pool of women's experience which is continually growing and changing as we act it out in our lives and interpret it for ourselves and each other in our conversation.'[1]

These words of Marie Tulip's opened the first issue of *Women-Church*, an Australian Journal of Feminist Studies in Religion, inaugurated in August 1987. They represent her assessment of Australian 'feminist theology' at that time and indicate that Australian feminist theologians have been latecomers to the international dialogue. Geographical isolation from the major centres and networks of this dialogue has been one contributing factor. Isolation of individual scholars in academic institutions resistant to feminist approaches to both religion and theology is another.

In the intervening years since 1987, feminist theology in Australia has, however, begun to assume a public face. It is being undertaken by individuals and small groups in centres separated from one another by the distances that characterize this vast and sparsely populated land of Australia. Its locations, too, are multifarious: study, ritual and spirituality groups; in homes and other spaces, some of which are women's spaces; in religious studies and theology departments in universities; and in theological schools. Communities of resistance are thus being formed as women and men are beginning to recognize that theology can only be done in truth when it is as inclusive of women's experience as it is of men's; and are undertaking feminist theologizing in these contexts. The strong web which such networking is beginning to create across our land provides an image of the complexity and the diversity of feminist theologizing, feminist theologizing and feminist religious thought and practice within the Australian context in recent years; and of the exciting and new stage that the future holds.

Weaving the web

Two recent Australian publications – *Claiming our Rites* and *Freedom and Entrapment*[2] – are indicative of some of the characteristics of this emerging new reality imaged as a web. They are both collections of essays and hence represent a broad sweep of Australian feminist scholars who are in critical dialogue with a range of religious traditions including the Christian theological tradition.

The origins of the two collections were in the fields of religious studies and Christian theology respectively, but the appearance of a number of contributors in both volumes indicates the networking that exists among Australian scholars across these fields. Indeed, the web encompasses feminist scholars, feminist thinkers in studies in religion, Christian theology, spirituality and spiritualities, and the history of women and religion in Australia. Such webbing has not been without tension, as differences among women have emerged in terms of their positioning of themselves in relation to patriarchal religions, new spiritualities, experience and tradition. It is, however, very visible in the contributions to *Women-Church* across its sixteen editions since 1987 and in the newly established network, Women Scholars in Religion and Theology, whose first directory appeared in 1993. It would be difficult and indeed undesirable to isolate a small part of this web and call it feminist theology distinct from the experience, thinking and writing that is emerging from these interconnected fields.

Two factors have contributed significantly to this characteristic of feminist religious thought in Australia. The first is small numbers and the dispersion of women scholars across the nation, which makes networking an important political strategy. The second is the lack of support for gender studies in religion in Australian universities[3] and for feminist studies in theology in its theological schools. Indeed, many scholars have been able to introduce one or two units into the course offerings across various institutions,[4] and advanced degree research students have been able to undertake research in these fields, but there is at present no institutional support for or recognition of gender or feminist studies in religion and theology as an area of specialization across our vast continent. The establishment of such centres will be a significant political break-through.

Australian women's unique cultural experiences, like those of their sisters across the globe, have become a powerful source for a new spiritual, theological and religious imagination, and a number of small journals have been the vehicles for women's reflection upon this experience. *Magdalene*, which was produced by Sydney women from 1973–1987, gave voice to 'a wide range of women's experience and their reflection on it in a context of meaning which assumes a feminist religious possibility'.[5] *Women-Church*, as already noted, had its origin in 1987, when *Magdalene* finished publication, and its co-editors, Hilary Carey and Erin White, wrote in the inaugural Editor's Introduction that they hoped that this journal would 'encourage the widest possible range of views and serve as a stimulus for further thought both about the divine and the particular journeys in religion taken by Australian women'.[6] Their hope has indeed been more than realized as this magazine links women across the continent and stimulates reflection, discussion and debate. July/August 1989 saw the first publication of *Voices from the Silence*, a National Ecumenical Women's Journal in which 'the most silent and silenced of our sisters could be heard'.[7] Even more recently, *Sounding Sophia*, the publication of the Sophia feminist spiritual centre in Adelaide, provided another avenue for women's religious and theological reflection on their experience.

Australian women's literature is providing another source for the Australian feminist theological and religious imagination. Veronica Brady, long time Associate Professor of English at the University of Western Australia, has consistently drawn upon Australian literature, but predominantly its male authors, as her theological source.[8] Her article in *Freedom and Entrapment*, however, sees a shift in focus to Australian women's writings[9] and together with Elaine Lindsay's contribution to *Claiming our Rites*[10] begins to redress the absence of women from discussions of Australian spirituality. Lindsay, in fact, allows the spirituality of the Australian novelist and mystic Barbara Hanrahan to speak through her own writing. This reflects her current doctoral research, *Rewriting God: Spirituality in Contemporary Australian Women's Fiction*, and points to the intersection between literature, spirituality and theology in the lives of a number of Australian women in a way which gives expression to unique Australian characteristics, especially relationship to the land, a significant factor shaping history and national identity. Lindsay provides a hint of this when she says that 'instead of adding to the sorry line of explorers and battlers who parade through malestream spirituality, Hanrahan wrote new myths set in domestic Australia, celebrating the courage needed to stay fresh and alive to the possibilities of each day'.[11]

Those Australian feminist theologians and religious scholars whose sources are ancient and contemporary texts within both Christianity and other religious traditions are participating in a feminist interpretative project which is international and multivocal.[12] As a result, they share the concerns of and are in dialogue with feminist scholars around the world engaged in the task of re-reading the grand narratives of not only Western religions but indigenous and Eastern religions as well. For the purpose of this essay, however, I will highlight the emerging contribution Australian feminist scholars are making to the re-interpretation of Christianity, since this is the dominant religious affiliation within Australia, the most recent Australian Bureau of Statistics citing that affiliation at 74% of the population.

Australian feminist biblical scholars are only in recent years beginning their contribution to the international dialogue. Dorothy Lee's article in *Claiming our Rites*[13] questions the impact for women's spirituality of beginning the interpretation of the sacred text with a hermeneutics of suspicion. In that same volume, I take account of Mary Daly's and Rosemary Radford Ruether's critique of androcentric christology and begin a re-reading of the Matthaean characterization of Jesus.[14] Veronica Lawson's essay in *Freedom and Entrapment* gives a taste of her doctoral research, which approaches the question of the genre of Luke-Acts from a feminist perspective.[15] Advanced research in biblical studies and many aspects of Christian theology is being undertaken by a number of students around the country. Most particularly, however, it is through courses in theological colleges and universities, publications in local journals and participation in workshops in many centres that women are weaving a strong web of reclamation of the biblical and Christian tradition across the continent.[16]

Maryanne Confoy, one of the editors of and contributors to *Freedom and Entrapment*, has taught for a number of years at one of Australia's theological colleges. From her perspective of personal development and ministry formation, she wrote recently of the 'tremendous demands' which the Australian system makes on its faculty members.[17] These demands are often greater on the small number of women teaching theology because of a lack of mentors, possible marginalization among a predominantly male faculty, additional workload if they wish to teach feminist studies in religion and theology, and the added demand of study for those still seeking the qualifications necessary to maintain their positions. Perhaps those demands will be lessened as the many women currently undertaking advanced degrees across the broad spectrum of theology, spirituality and religion take their places in theological colleges, universities, spirituality centres and other centres of learning. Communities of resistance within theological colleges may be further strengthened as women enter strategic positions in the wake of Dorothy Lee's recent appointment as Professor of New Testament at The Uniting Church Theological Hall in Melbourne. These are signs of hope for the future strengthening of the web of resistance.

This web is, however, very fragile in a number of places. The editors of *Claiming our Rites* noted that studies in religion is a peculiarly 'Western' activity and that 'the absence of a paper of Aboriginal authorship in this collection is itself a marker of the limits of a field dependent on conventions which constrain to the point of exclusion'.[18] The very title of Anne Pattel-Gray's contribution to *Freedom and Entrapment*, 'Not yet Tiddas (Sisters): An Aboriginal womanist critique of Australian Church feminism', suggests that theology, too, is no stranger to the same type of exclusion when undertaken, as it has been in Australia, by predominantly white women of European descent.[19] The spirituality of indigenous Australian women is, however, not only being expressed but also heard and recognized by other Australians through their literature, their music and dance and their art.[20] The challenge remains for Australian feminists to allow the 'theoretical and practical space' for the voices of Aboriginal women to be heard in their 'difference and dissent'. Likewise, Australia's geographical location on the edge of the Pacific rim and the southern tip of Asia has largely been ignored in feminist theological discourse and it opens up an area of dialogue for the future.

The lack of institutional support for feminist studies in religion and theology in Australia indicates, however, that the voice of women generally in all the 'difference and dissent' is being excluded from Australian theologizing. The significant impact of this exclusion on the history of these studies has not, however, always been recognized. In the beginning of the current women's movement, Barbara Thiering was a public voice for the movement's impact on Australian women's practice of religion, especially Christianity.[21] The personal testimony of women who were students in her courses at the University of Sydney indicates that she inspired many who would become political activists in their churches, especially the Anglican church. She herself, however, was marginalized by that church. Other stories of the genderization of Australian churches have likewise been told.[22] As Australian women appropriated feminism and its impact on theology and religion by way of the publications from the United

States of America and Europe which reached these shores during the 1970s and 1980s, they became more aware of their virtual exclusion from the path of theological education unless they were training for ministry in those denominations which ordained women. Many women turned, therefore, to other disciplines – philosophy, literature and sociology.

These women have taken religion and religious traditions into the universities as research topics in a variety of disciplines, leading to a strengthening of the secular and religious in those institutions. In Australia generally, this bond has not been strong, and Australian feminist studies and feminist critical theory have given little or no attention to religion and theology. The relationship has not, however, been hostile, as the debate – Is it worthwhile for women to pour their energies into a feminist movement within Christianity? – at the first conference of the National Foundation of Australian Women indicated. There are signs that another strand of our web might be strengthened as Australian women become more competent in the analyses of theological and religious traditions using multi-disciplinary perspectives, and as Women's Studies departments become more secure within Australian universities. The dialogue between Australian feminists shows signs of becoming more diverse so that it will include religion and theology. This expanded vision can only strengthen feminist theologizing in Australia and ground it more firmly in its geographical location.

Lack of ecclesial support for Australian women's theologizing has, on the other hand, led to the development of strong political networks of women within the three major Christian denominations and ecumenically across these denominations. These networks have become the locations of some of our most significant feminist theologizing and strategizing. Within the Catholic tradition, and particularly during the 1970s and 1980s, women in religious congregations had been given the opportunity for theological education, often overseas, where they were influenced by feminist theologians in the United States and Europe. This led them, through the Conference of Major Superiors of Women and Men Religious, to initiate the WATAC (Women and the Australian Church) project, which began with a survey of the roles of women in church and society but was intended to be a consciousness-raising activity for all in the Catholic Church. The organization, through a varied history, continues today as a grass-roots women's group within the Catholic tradition providing the space in which women can explore their theological and spiritual traditions.[23] Much of the feminist energy of Anglican women in Australia during the 1980s was directed to the Movement of the Ordination of Women (MOW), both its political strategies and theological and spiritual underpinning.[24] Their goal was attained at the end of 1992 with the ordination of women in a number of Australian dioceses.[25] The Uniting Church women who had access to ordination in their tradition only recently established FUN (Feminist Uniting Network). From the first National Conference on Women in the Uniting Church in Australia in 1990[26] came the Last Supper Project, which commissioned a painting of the Last Supper which would include women, highlighting another expression of women's theologizing. Also from the project has come the book *A Place at the Table: Women at the Last Supper*, which explores artistic and theological aspects of the theme.[27]

One significant point of focus for Australian feminist theology has been the biennial conference, organized by the above groups with Sydney Women-Church since 1989. They symbolize the ecumenical nature of feminist theology in Australia with the degree of co-operation in local centres reflecting the ecclesial history of the states or cities in which groups are located. This ecumenism is also visible in The Australian Feminist Theology Foundation, established in 1992 as a strategic action to encourage feminist theology and support it financially; to challenge patriarchal structures, theology and practice; to develop inclusive and participatory liturgy; and 'to promote feminist theology as a rigorous, analytical and intellectual pilgrimage of significance for the whole community'.[28]

Conclusion

Australia's ecclesial and national histories, its geographical location, dispersion of peoples across a vast land and, no doubt, many other factors, have meant that only recently have Australian feminist theological voices been raised aloud in the public arena. The brief resonances of the small number of these voices that have been heard in this article indicate that Australian feminist theologians and religionists stand on the edge of new possibilities for the future. They will be challenged to provide the space for differences among women – ethnic, racial, socio-economic, denominational, sexual orientation and many others – to be heard theologically both in dialogue and dissent. The future will also call for a strengthening of the web linking women in their dispersion across vast distances of this continent and into the Pacific and Asia. The institutionalization of Australian feminist theology and studies of religion without their co-optation into patriarchal structures will require skilful political strategies so that energies can be concentrated. Local sources will inform a more specifically Australian feminist theology, while the addressing of international religious and theological concerns will continue. The weaving of a strong web across this continent has begun. Its fragile strands need to be strengthened and its connections with the wider global network developed, but there are many who will undertake these tasks.

In an article such as this, I am aware how the limitations of space prevent a real acknowledgment of the breadth and strength of the strong web of Australian feminist theology. So I would like to dedicate the article to all those women engaged in Australian feminist theology who are contributing and will contribute in so many different ways to the weaving of a much stronger web for the future.

Notes

1. Marie Tulip, 'Dimensions of Feminist Theology in Australia', *Women-Church* 1, 1987, 4.
2. Morny Joy and Penelope Magee (eds.), *Claiming our Rites: Studies in Religion by Australian Women Scholars*, Adelaide 1994; Maryanne Confoy and Dorothy Lee (eds.), *Freedom and Entrapment*, Melbourne 1995.
3. As noted by Joy and Magee, *Claiming our Rites* (n. 2), xii.
4. Alan Bayley, 'Women and Religion Courses in Australia', *Australian Religion Studies Review* 1.1, 1988, 53–60; Erin White, 'Webbing', *Women-Church* 3, 1988, 5. There has been no recent survey, and the numbers and extent of course offerings would certainly have increased significantly.
5. Tulip, 'Dimensions of Feminist Theology' (n.1), 4.
6. Hilary Carey and Erin White, 'Editor's Introduction', *Women-Church* 1, 1987, 3. The contribution of Erin White and Marie Tulip to Australian feminist theology is also evident in their co-authored book, *Knowing Otherwise: Feminism, Women and Religion*, Melbourne 1990.
7. Sandra Brown, 'Voices', *Voices from the Silence* 1, 1989, 1.
8. Veronica Brady, *A Crucible of Prophets: Australians and the Question of God*, Australian and New Zealand Studies in Theology and Religion, Sydney 1981; and *Caught Up in the Draught: On Contemporary Australian Culture and Society*, Sydney 1994.
9. Veronica Brady, 'Every Christian in Her Own Place: Women's Writing and Theological Understanding', in *Freedom and Entrapment* (n. 2), 63–78.
10. Elaine Lindsay, 'A Mystic in her Garden: Spirituality and the Fiction of Barbara Hanrahan', in *Claiming our Rites* (n. 2), 19–36.
11. Ibid., 30.
12. The number of contributions to the two recent publications that belong in this category are too numerous to detail here.
13. Dorothy A. Lee, 'Reclaiming the Sacred Text: Christian Feminism and Spirituality', in *Claiming our Rites* (n. 2), 79–98.
14. Elaine Mary Wainwright, 'Wisdom is Justified by her Deeds: Claiming the Jesus-Myth', *Claiming our Rites* (n. 2), 57–78. See also, *Towards a Feminist Critical Reading of the Gospel according to Matthew*, BZNW 60, Berlin 1991; ead., 'The Gospel

of Matthew', in *Searching the Scriptures, Volume Two: A Feminist Commentary*, ed. Elisabeth Schüssler Fiorenza, New York and London 1994, 635–77.

15. Veronica Lawson, 'Scraps of Sustenance for the Journey out of Patriarchy: Acts 1:1–14 in Feminist Perspective', in *Freedom and Entrapment* (n. 2), 149–64.

16. The work of Christine Burke, *Through a Woman's Eyes: Encounters with Jesus*, Burwood, Victoria 1989, makes a significant contribution to this process.

17. Mary Anne Confoy, 'Women's Impact on Theological Education', in *Discovering an Australian Theology*, ed. Peter Malone, Homebush, NSW 1988, 147–161.

18. *Claiming our Rites* (n. 2), xx.

19. *Freedom and Entrapment* (n. 2), 165–192. I have added the translation of 'Tiddas' to the title for international readers.

20. By way of example see Sally Morgan, *My Place*, Freemantle 1987; Miriam-Rose Ungunmerr-Baumann, *Australian Stations of the Cross*, Melbourne 1984; Rosemary Crumlin and Anthony Knight (eds.), *Aboriginal Art and Spirituality*, North Blackburn, Vic 1991.

21. Barbara Thiering, *Created Second? Aspects of Women's Liberation in Australia*, Adelaide 1973; and ead. (ed.), *Deliver us from Eve: Essays on Australian Women and Religion*, Sydney 1977.

22. Margaret Ann Franklin (ed.), *The Force of the Feminine*, Sydney 1986; Margaret Ann Franklin and Ruth Sturmey Jones (eds.), *Opening the Cage: Stories of Church and Gender*, Sydney 1987.

23. Angela Coco, *Women and the Australian Church: Project or Proclamation*, BA Hons. Thesis submitted to the Department of Studies in Religion at the University of Queensland 1991, studies the movement and its history.

24. See Muriel Porter, *Women in the Church: The Great Ordination Debate in Australia*, Ringwood, Vic. 1989, as one insight into this story. The local and national magazines of MOW also contain the stories and the theology of this long struggle.

25. In the subsequent year a new organization, Ordination of Catholic Women (OCW), came into existence and held its first conference in Canberra in 1994 just months after the May 1994 papal letter *Ordinatio Sacralis*.

26. Elizabeth Wood Ellem (ed.), *The Church Made Whole*, Melbourne 1990, is a publication of proceedings.

27. Judi Fisher and Janet Wood (eds.), *A Place at the Table: Women at the Last Supper*, Melbourne 1993.

28. Summarized and quoted from the brochure of the Foundation.

Between Colonialism and Inculturation: Feminist Theologies in Africa

Teresia M. Hinga

Introduction

In 1989, approximately seventy African women met in Ghana with the aim of initiating a forum through which they could research, analyse and reflect upon their experiences in the tremendous variety of contexts in which they live. After suitable debate and deliberation, this group decided to call itself 'The Circle of Concerned African Women Theologians'.

Whereas it would be inaccurate to claim that before 1989 an African women's theological voice was absent in Africa,[1] the 1989 meeting was a turning-point in the emergence of a more formal and probably more systematic 'feminist' theology on the continent. Through this convocation and its consequent activities, the diverse struggles of African women and how these have been shaped and influenced by the historical, religious, cultural and theological milieux in which they live become more crystallized and visible.

An analysis of the goals[2] of this circle of women, then, becomes a viable framework through which to describe the nature and direction of the feminist theological voice in Africa, a voice which two decades ago was conspicuous by its absence. Our task here is to highlight the key features of this nascent theological voice.

The clues in the name and the will to arise

Perhaps the best place to start our analysis is to examine more closely the implications of the very title the women chose to designate themselves.

What clues does the name 'Circle of Concerned African Women Theologians' give us for understanding the nature and the direction of the women's theological voice in Africa? Several points are pertinent here.

First, we note that the women seem to have deliberately avoided labelling their project 'feminist', despite the fact that feminist theology had already been flourishing under that label in the West for at least a decade. The significance of the seeming avoidance of the label 'feminist' becomes clear when we consider that, by definition, feminist theology is contextual, seeking to give analytical weight specifically to the experiences of women and the injustices they suffer particularly because of sexism. Despite the commitment by feminists to make the experiences of women the primary source and rationale for their theology, it is also recognized that there is no such thing as 'generic women' whose 'generic experiences' can become the subject-matter of 'generic feminist theology'. Women's experiences are so diverse that to speak of a monolithic feminist theology is seemingly absurd.[3]

The awareness of the problem implicit in thinking of feminist theology as monolithic led African women to conclude that their experiences are sufficiently different from those of women elsewhere to warrant a distinct analysis and a distinct label.[4]

The women also seem to have been careful to include the term 'Africa' in their self-designation, drawing attention to two aspects of their project. First, they insisted that the cultural context from which they speak and to which they speak is itself distinct from other cultural contexts, particularly the Western one, and that this distinct cultural context shapes their theological agenda significantly. Secondly, they pointed to their distinct history as Africans, a history which has been irrevocably marked by colonialism. The inclusion of the term Africa then was their attempt to name the cultural and social-historical location which is the springboard for their theology.

The significance of the term African in the women's self-definition becomes even more poignant when we consider that the primary concern of African women has been their lack of voice in theological as well as in other discourses. This situation has largely been attributable to the legacy of imperialism and paternalism that has characterized the relationship between Westerners and Africans. The assumption for a long time has been that Africans are to be guided, represented and spoken on behalf of, since they are either unwilling or unable to do so for themselves. African women have been double victims of this legacy, since even when it is considered viable to listen to Africa, the voice of African women is still unheard, since it is assumed that their voice is included in that of men. It is the injustice implicit in this enforced silence that led Oduyoye, the pioneer and leading African feminist theologian, to lament:

> As long as men and Western strangers continue to write exclusively about Africa, African women will continue to be represented as if they were dead! (Oduyoye, 1992, 10).

Considering this injustice, then, part of African women's struggle is against the imperialism implicit in the efforts of others, particularly Westerners, to represent them, a struggle which they share with male theologians. For African women, however, their critique of Western paternalism includes the critique of Western women in so far as they, too, may presume to speak on their behalf. African women insist that the right to speak for themselves is a necessary condition for their emancipation and must be respected by all. As Ifi, a leading African feminist, insists:

> African women can ignore historical and cultural differences only at their own peril in view of the damage done already by colonialism and still being inflicted by neo-colonialism and Western feminist imperialism (Ifi, 1987, 8).

Realizing also that years of forced silence may in fact have led women to become entrenched in apathy and seeming acquiescence with the various oppressions, African feminist theology today is both a protest against the forced silence, and also a wake-up call to African women to rise and fight against the forces of injustice that surround them. The commitment to speak and act for themselves is well captured in the title of their first book, *The Will to Arise*, comprising papers discussed in the 1989 convocation. In her introduction to the book, Oduyoye interprets the title as symbolic of the women's vision of themselves. As she put it:

> *The Will to Arise* is the voice of African women theologians. It is grounded in the challenges of scripture and results from a new wave of change. African women reading the scriptures have begun to see that God's call for them is not passive. It is compelling and compulsory. It is a call to action and wholeness that challenges the will and the intellect (*Will to Arise*, 1).

The third pertinent aspect of the women's description of their project is their insistence that they are a circle of concerned African women. This drew attention to the fact that contrary to stereotypes of African women as either unaware or indifferent to their oppression, they are conscious, capable and willing to deal with issues of moral concern. It is such concerns that they consider a challenge both to their will and their intellect as they consciously and conscientiously strive to analyse the web of oppression[5] under which they live. Not only are the women aware of the issues confronting them and the continent as a whole, but they also feel compelled to act towards the resolution of these issues.

One can infer, then, that though the African women have not given themselves the technical title of 'feminists', they are nonetheless involved in a project that is similar to that of women in other contexts, particularly in the Third World. As Ursula King remarks in her anthology of feminist theology from the Third World, African women's theology is:

> Feminist theology (which) puts emphasis on praxis and action . . . It sees theology as an ongoing process and is committed to life, justice and freedom from oppression . . . It is not theology as reified but is (primarily concerned with concrete issues) of life as experienced . . . (King, 1994, 16).

African women's theological concerns

What then are the concrete issues that concern African women as feminist theologians?

The foregoing analysis reveals that the primary concern of African women is their desire to break out of their enforced silence. Claiming their right to speak for themselves, the women began the process of naming their pain, and isolated various areas of concern; however, they prioritized the analysis of the implications of religion and culture for their lives. Thus, the goal for the first phase of their project would be to

> concentrate efforts on producing literature from the basis of religion and culture to enrich the critical study of religion in Africa (Oduyoye, 1990, 1).

Consequently, the circle embarked on a sustained, systematic research and publication initiative, focussing on the critical analysis of the impact of culture and religion in their lives.

This project addresses several dimensions of the problem of religion and culture in Africa. First, there is the issue of diversity. To speak of religion and culture in Africa is to speak of at least three major heritages, namely, indigenous African religion, Christianity and Islam. These have, either cumulatively or independently, significantly influenced the definition of women in Africa. In analysing the impact of culture and religion on their lives, African women have had to reckon with the diversity of concepts and interpretations of womanhood that are implicit in these traditions.[6] It is this cultural pluralism which made it methodologically imperative for the women to adopt what they called a dialogical approach. Their aim was not only to ensure a more inclusive forum that would respect this essential pluralism of the continent, but also to set an example of how best to deal with the issue of cultural diversity which often occasions conflict in Africa. Thus, as they argued:

> The circle is designed to focus on the three main religions in Africa: it will be a symbol of Africa's recognition of the necessity of the dialogical approach to religious and cultural plurality in Africa and the practical consequences it has for peace in our communities (Oduyoye, 1990, 2).

Secondly, in navigating their critical route through the issue of religion and culture, the women also have to deal with the historical reality of cultural imperialism implicit in the imposition of the Western way of life in Africa, particularly the imposition of Western religion. Here, African women are engaged in a two-pronged struggle. On the one hand they are fighting along with African men against such cultural imperialism and are therefore critical of agendas and proposals made by Westerners about the viability or otherwise of aspects of African culture.[7]

At the same time, however, aware that African culture itself is not immune to sexism, the women's critique is also addressed to African men who tend to idealize it. Some men accuse women of raising false alarms about the alleged oppression and sexism in Africa, while others accuse African women of uncritically imitating disgruntled Western women who in turn are stereotyped as unnecessarily belligerent, anti-men and anti-family, attitudes which are considered un-African and therefore unworthy of self-respecting African women.

Such attitudes of trivialization and denial are not only found in the secular society in Africa but are also manifest in the church and even in emerging 'Third World' theologies of liberation. Indeed, it is the experience of such trivialization of their plight within the established theological forums which led initially to what has been referred to as the irruption of women.[8] The women's critique is therefore legitimately directed to African male theologians for thus participating in the silencing of women: In the women's words:

> What Third World theology says to Western theology is that their voices must be heard because experiences vary . . . it is this same word that African women say to African men theologians . . . we live in the same continent but . . . there are many Africas . . . the Africa of the rich and the Africa of the poor . . . the Africa of men who command and that of

women who obey . . . To all we wish to say that new factor has arrived on the theological scene in the form of African women who write theology and who have covenanted to articulate the concerns of women . . . all who call themselves prophetic theologians of Africa will have to reckon with this! (Oduyoye, 1990, 41).

While the immediate occasion for the outburst of women was the use of sexist language in theological forums, the women perceived this as a symptom of a broader problem of sexism and patriarchy even in African cultures. Realizing this, using a critical feminist hermeneutics of suspicion which refuses an *a priori* idealization of any culture, African women embarked on a systematic evaluation of African culture in the light of sexism.[9]

Thirdly, although most of the women involved in the circle are Christians, their critical hermeneutics of religion and culture also involves them in an analysis of the decisively ambiguous impact of Christianity in their lives. On the one hand they have noted that Christianity has participated in the oppression of women, since it has functioned to legitimize colonialism, racism and sexism. On the other hand, it is noted that many African women have appropriated for themselves the gospel of liberty implicit in Christianity as a strong motivating force in their struggle for liberation.

Recognizing the practice of injustices in church and society as a sinful betrayal of the vision of Jesus who laid a foundation for a human society characterized by equality, freedom and justice, African Christian women see their task as a prophetic one of unmasking and challenging such sinful practices and structures of injustice. Thus, they see no contradiction, as some Western feminists do, in being both feminist and Christian.

The women's critique of Christianity also involves them in a critical re-reading and re-evaluating of the role of the Bible as a source for Christian theology. Again, here they differ from some of their Western sisters, who see the Bible as so irredeemably warped by patriarchy that it is useless as a resource for women seeking liberation from sexism. While rejecting sexist and patriarchal exegeses and hermeneutics as sinful, women have continued critically to read the Bible and reflect upon it for inspiration and as a theological resource.

We may conclude, therefore, that a primary concern of African women's theology is to voice their protest against sexism and its roots in religion and culture. This protest is initially two-pronged, since it is directed at both African religion and culture and Christianity.

Conclusions: the enduring challenges

While the above is a summary of key themes in the emergent African feminist theology so far, it is not an exhaustive account, since African feminist theology is a theology still en route. Thus it would be premature to say that we have captured all that it could become! Suffice it here in conclusion to highlight some of the enduring issues and challenges which the women have courageously committed themselves to address, despite the many odds facing them.

First, African women have committed themselves to create a theology that is not just about women but is also of women. Now, considering that the majority of African women are so embroiled in daily struggles for survival as to make their involvement in 'formal' theology impossible, the circle of theologians must be consistent in its efforts to include the experiences of the so-called grass-roots women in their theological agenda. The enduring challenge is for the women theologians to resist privileging experiences of elite women as normative for theology. They must also guard against the danger of silencing the masses of women by an *a priori* presumption to speak on their behalf. This necessitates constant dialogue with all women, whatever their social status. Only then can the emerging theology become genuinely representative, echoing the concerns of all women, despite the bewildering variety of their experiences.

Secondly, emerging African feminist theology so far is largely a product of Christian women, particularly from the mainstream missionary churches. Considering, however, that Africa is not a cultural or religious monolith, the Christian women's voice is not the only possible theological voice there. The evolving African feminist theology is then challenged to honour its commitment not to privilege Christianity at the expense of other religious traditions. Thus it must consider the insights and experiences of non-Christian women, particularly Muslim women, since Islam is a major force in African women's lives. It will also need to take seriously the experiences of African women, who, undeterred by Christian propaganda against African religion, continue to practise forms of African spirituality as healers, priestesses and prophetesses. African feminist theology must also take the experiences of those who do their theology on the fringes of Christianity. This includes the multitudes of women members of independent churches, many of which, it will be remembered, started in protest against the marginalization of Africans and their spirituality by missionaries and their theological discourse, and were often dismissed as heretical or culpably syncretistic. Given the women's commitment to a dialogical approach to the issue of religious pluralism, African feminist theology may thus be compelled to shift from the prevailing christocentric model of theology in order to do justice to the variety of African women's spiritualities and religious experiences.

Thirdly, although in this first phase of their project women are primarily engaged in a legitimate feminist critique of religion and culture in Africa, it is also important to remember the equally urgent issues of survival that the African women are facing. For African feminist theology to avoid the danger of reification, it has to be consistently engaged with issues of women's political empowerment and economic justice, issues that are at the root of many of the problems that African women continue to endure. Since African women's theology is committed to play an advocacy role on behalf of women, it is challenged to persist in seeking practical solutions to the many problems that women face. Such a visible and unwavering engagement with issues of women's survival will be a significant measure of the continued credibility of feminist theology as it evolves on the continent.

Last but not least, though African feminist theology is context-specific and focussed, for reasons discussed earlier, the question persists as to the relationship African women perceive themselves to have with other feminist theologians elsewhere. Here, it seems, the women think it possible to envisage a future marked by their genuine solidarity with all those of good will who strive for a more just global community. Their enduring commitment and challenge is to bring practical gifts and contributions to the process of healing and reconstruction, not only of their battered continent but also of a battered world.

Bibliography

Amadiume Ifi, *Male Daughters and Female Husbands. Gender and Sex in African Society*, London 1987.
Ursula King, *Feminist Theology From The Third World: A Reader*, Maryknoll 1994.
Amba Oduyoye and R. A. Kanyoro (eds.), *The Will to Arise: Women, Tradition and the Church in Africa*, Maryknoll 1992.
Amba Oduyoye, *Talitha Qumi: The Proceedings of the Convocation of African Women Theologians*, Ibadan 1990.
E. Vicky Spelman, *Inessential Woman: Problems of Exclusion in Feminist Thought*, Boston 1988.

Notes

1. For details of events that led to the crystallization of the women's theological voice, see Mercy Oduyoye, 'Reflections from a Third World Perspective: Women's Experience and Liberation Theology', in King, 1994, 22–33.

2. The Circle of Women committed themselves initially to a seven-year research and publication project. They planned to convene again in 1996 to take stock of their achievements and map out future strategies. For details of the Circle and its goals, see Oduyoye, 1990, 1–7.

3. The issue of the diversity of women's experiences and its implications for the global feminist project is the subject matter of Spelman, 1988.

4. Similar conclusions have been reached by Black women in North America, who call their version of theology 'womanist', while Hispanic women have labelled theirs 'Mujerista theology'.

5. The phrase 'web of oppression' is used in African feminist discourse to describe the multiple and interlocking levels of oppression that they face as result of racism, classism, colonialism and sexism, a situation similar to that of all so-called 'Third World women'.

6. Consider, for example, the difficulties women may face in their attempt at critical evaluation of the practice of polygamy, given that this practice is considered legitimate in Islam and African religion, while it is outlawed in Christianity.

7. See, for instance, the heated controversies surrounding the interpretations of practices like polygamy and female circumcision as discussed for example in the preface to Ifi, 1987, and compare this with Oduyoye, 1990, 45.

8. For details of the events that led to the irruption of women see Oduyoye in King, 1994, 23ff.

9. See the essays in the Circle's first anthology, *The Will to Arise*.

Feminist Theology in Europe: Between Movement and Academic Institutionalization

Monika Jakobs

The development of European feminist theology is closely bound up with the reception of American feminist theology: above all the early publications of Mary Daly and Rosemary Radford Ruether also played a key role for the left wing of the European discussion. Of course these ideas did not fall on ground that was unprepared. In the Catholic Church there had been a sensitivity to the question of women at least since Vatican II, primarily in connection with priestly office; in addition there was the secular women's movement of the 1970s, which increasingly led women theologians to put questions to their existing church and theology. This development has been documented elsewhere.[1]

The present spectrum of feminist theology in Europe is wide, and there are many forms of its institutionalization. Posts related to women have become a firm part of church educational establishments; there are posts for women in the churches, and feminist theologians teach in universities. There are archives and a great many national and international networks.

Although there has been much movement and some things have been achieved, the positive appearances disguise the difficulty which still exists in implementing the substance of feminist theology and the fragility of the support for such projects in terms of material and personnel. Although feminist theology has become a fact which can no longer be ignored in theological and church discussion, it is still a 'rebellion on the frontier'.[2]

Furthermore, there are enormous differences between the confessions, and between individual European regions and countries. European feminist theologians are pastors in the Swedish state church; in Rumania, as members of a Hungarian minority, they are attempting to establish an independent theological college with no resources; they try to work on a project of feminist theology in addition to looking after a family or holding down a job; they are Orthodox academic teachers in Greece, Catholic collaborators in an interim feminist project in the Netherlands or Protestant theologians and pastors in Switzerland. The enormous difference in personal situations is an indication of the different cultural, national, political and material conditions in Europe. This general framework also contributes towards shaping feminist theology.

Theological research into women or feminist theology?

The very varied 'landscape' of Europe makes it impossible to offer a regional treatment of feminist theology in a continuum of development. Such a classification would inevitably start from a standpoint of arrogance, which regarded its own position as the most progressive or most balanced.

Nevertheless, it is helpful to note some points of substance. One line which has developed through feminist theology is the question of feminism. In some countries like France or Spain, there is a tremendous amount of scepticism about this term, and women theologians are somewhat cautious about calling themselves feminist.[3] Behind this probably lies the fear of being misunderstood as separatist and un-feminine. Accordingly, one important voice of feminist theology in France is the association 'Femmes et Hommes en Eglise', which is also open to men. Its key word is 'partenariat', partnership.[4]

Nevertheless, one must raise the question whether feminist theology is not more than a movement for equal rights in the churches, asking where its hermeneutical quality lies, in other words asking how the perspective on theology and its content is changing. Here the women's movement in the churches has not stopped at calling for equal rights for women; it has recognized that the full participation of women in the formation of theological theory has far-reaching consequences for the self-understanding of theology as a science and for its content. Hedwig Meyer-Wilmes writes: 'The issue here is the development of the women's question as a problem of the status of women in theology and church in the direction of a plea for an alternative understanding of theology and church.'[5] Accordingly, feminist theology does not define itself in terms of so-called 'women's themes' or researchers who happen to be feminine, but seeks a new understanding of theology.

The discussion of feminist research has provoked important questions for sociology.[6] What is called for is no less than an 'alternative paradigm of research'.[7] This must involve 'deliberate partisanship'[8] rather than pseudo-objectivity, and the obligation of academic studies to engage in liberating praxis (in this case the women's movement). These postulates are much discussed among women scholars and as yet there is no agreement over them.

Hedwig Meyer-Wilmes has transferred these demands to feminist theology. In her view, what is constitutive of feminist theology is 'to understand itself as part of a movement and reflection on it'.[9] Although feminist theology, understood in this way, represents 'a break with theology as it has understood itself so far',[10] at the same time it needs to establish itself in faculties.

The new element in this hermeneutics is the insight already contributed by political theology and theology of liberation that theology is always partisan, whether or not it intends to be. Therefore it is necessary to formulate this partisan nature and to provide a basis for it.

The problem in such an approach lies in the point of reference: to what praxis does feminist theology relate? Is there a binding view of what is to be understood by women's liberation?

The issue is the dialectic between theory and praxis or the contextuality which feminist theology claims for itself; here it should be remembered that these two poles are not static entities.

In other words, feminist theology always relates to specific individuals, to real political, historical and social situations. This connection must always remain visible; otherwise theology degenerates into ideology.

Autonomy or institutionalization?

What are the contexts of feminist theology?

Mary Daly remarked that patriarchy seemed to be everywhere.[11] If one shares this shattering insight, it is no longer possible to be involved in existing structures. Daly has often been accused of separatism, and she has tried to distance herself as far as possible from patriarchal institutions and to be autonomous. This has been and is a deterrent to many women, yet the notion of total inward and outward independence has retained its attraction, perhaps not coincidentally in phases in which an individual life has not yet been planned out, or there seems to be no hope of concrete possibilities for work and earning in society.[12] Is autonomy the only possible way of engaging in feminist scholarship without being commandeered, with people one chooses oneself, with a combination of life and work, and freedom from the constraints of the economics of work?[13]

In reality it has been possible to meet these expectations of autonomous forms of life only in part. The self-exploitation of the zero tariff has often taken the place of freedom from the pressures of the world of work; the lack of a line between private life and work becomes a burden. In time it has proved that autonomous life and work is a possibility which is open only to some. Autonomy understood in this way is inappropriate as the sole future perspective of feminist theology.

However, pragmatic reasons are not the only decisive ones. Women theologians identify with their church. So their criticism of structures and substances with a masculine stamp goes with the effort to work and be effective within institutions. Here feminist theology is understood as an indispensable element of Christian theology generally. This option means recognizing formal qualifications, observing the existing 'rules of the game', gaining conviction through work, acting tactfully.

In many universities in German-speaking countries and in the Netherlands there are regular teaching posts for feminist theology. About a decade ago these were fought for by a large number of women students. But if we look more closely, we have to note that such posts often do not lead to a demonstration of competence, that because they rotate they are taken lightly by the students (who also take into account the possible importance of a discipline for a final examination), that they are badly paid, and must continually be fought for all over again. Doctoral and post-doctoral students whose subjects relate to feminist theology must fear that the choice of their topic will damage their careers, and will have to take some time and trouble to seek support from their faculty so that they can go through the formal process without friction. A particularly critical eye is cast on their works.

However, a connection with the university is important for academic feminist theology in particular, and not just for pragmatic reasons (because research costs money or so that the relevant infrastructure can be used). The institution is by no means to be looked at only from the perspective of rituals of patriarchal scholarship; there is also the pressure – which is positive in the last resort – to assert oneself in academic discourse, since for all its inconveniences, it provides protection from one-dimensional thinking and spiritual and intellectual isolation. In the long term it is important for all innovative theologies, including feminist theology, to participate in the academic tradition in order to help to shape it.

However, the institutionalization of feminist theology does not take place only at the universities. A more important but similar point is the work of the churches' women's associations and educational institutions. A look at their announcements and programmes confirms this. This grass-roots work is of particular importance, since it brings together theory and praxis and earths feminist discussion.

Rebellion on the frontier

A good example of the difficulties of academic institutionalization is the policy of filling academic chairs, and the 'fate' of academic chairs created specifically for theological women's research, above all in Germany.

When Elisabeth Gössmann wrote her Habilitation thesis in 1963, people were not yet speaking of feminist theology. She describes her experience: ' . . .whereas male colleagues who had trained at the same Institute of the University of Munich were receiving calls to theological chairs in the Republic in hordes at this time, regardless of whether they had completed their Habilitation or not even begun it. For many of them a professorship was just a step on the way to the episcopate.'[4] The obstacle for her was competition from clerical males and the fact that at this time she seemed a complete exception as a Catholic woman theologian with academic qualifications. Nevertheless, in retrospect she also sees a feminist component here: 'In order to obtain the *imprimatur*, my early books on women had to incorporate the hierarchy of the man over the women in marriage into the text.'[5] Despite her recognized academic achievements, Elisabeth Gössmann was never given a chair in Germany, and since 1965 has taught in Japan.

In 1991 the information that Silvia Schroer, who occupied first place on the list for the Tübingen chair of Old Testament Introduction, had been refused permission to teach by the local bishop responsible, Walter Kasper, caused a stir. The precise reasons are very hard to discover. In a commentary on the event Lucia Scherzberg suggested that Silvia Schroer was not 'a feminist theologian pursued by the church', but the 'victim of the hesitation of a German institutional church to take bold steps in the face of the touchy Catholic fundamentalist groups . . . '[6] These circles had taken offence at a popular article by Schroer on mariology in a Swiss church journal. After the event, an exegetical article in which Silvia Schroer put forward the argument that Mark 1.10f. refers to the dove as a messenger bird of the old Near Eastern goddess of love as the occasion for the failure to appoint her.[17] It is impossible to discover the circumstances surrounding her rejection.

The liturgical scholar and ecumenist Teresa Berger could not take up the professorial chairs offered her either in Fribourg, Switzerland, in Bochum or in Bonn, as she was not given the church's permission to teach. Granted, it is conceded that the faculties, too, had made formal mistakes, but in an opinion from Rome it was said that she did not have the right 'mentalité catholique'.[18] Perhaps the reason for this was her ecumenical qualifications (Anglican licentiate, Protestant title of Master and Catholic diploma)? Here too the proceedings were obscure and wearisome. Rome later said that an article about the idea of Christ as feminine had hardened suspicions expressed earlier. Here, however, Berger was not postulating such femininity, but the problem of claiming the maleness of Jesus for theological arguments.[19]

In 1993, an appointment to a chair of feminist theology in 1993 was announced. This appointment has yet to be made. Two aspects should be stressed in this extremely complicated process. A year later, when there was already a list of potential calls, the chair was described again, 'with a new dedication of the chair'.[20] After conversations with the Catholic Church the list of potential calls was abandoned. The new description runs, '. . . and theological research into women'. What theological discipline is meant by this still remains open.

A second specific feature of this appointment was a failure to note the distinguished theologian Elisabeth Schüssler Fiorenza on the list of potential calls. One wonders what role was played here by a special comment in which the head of 'Arbeits- und Forschungstelle Feminist-ische Theologie', Lucia Scherzberg, postulated 'emancipation' from the 'American big sister'.[21] The theologian concerned, Elisabeth Schüssler Fiorenza, warns against the tendency towards 'privatization and per-sonalization in the case of the "chair of Feminist Theology in the University of Münster"'.[22] Certainly in the cases mentioned, particular factors which cannot readily be seen from outside played a role. But it is extremely problematical to link such rejections to individual statements. The impression one gets is rather that feminist theologians are not wanted as professors, so reasons are found not to appoint them. For me, this is an expression of a church-political strategy which pays far less attention to feminist theology than is to be feared or hoped for; rather, it is stamped by an anxiety in an embattled and questioned situation in the societies of Europe from which the church is gradually vanishing.

A second attempt at interpretation. In Germany a professorship at a university carries with it high social status and material support. If a professorship really is something, the mechanisms which exclude women can be understood particularly well. That is also evident from the first professorial chair in feminist theology in Nijmegen, which was occupied by Catharina Halkes between 1983 and 1986 and is now occupied by Atahlya Brenner.[23] The chair itself was unsalaried, and the only pay was the post of lecturer to which it was attached. Nevertheless, many signals went out from the concerns over this chair, especially the integration of feminist theology into the regular curriculum of study. There is now a second major chair of feminist theology in Groningen, the permanent holder of which is Riet Bons-Storm. The effectiveness of Dutch feminist theology is above all due to the strong network there, e.g. the IWFT, the Inter-University Working Group for Feminism and Theology, or inter-disciplinary research projects at some universities.

European feminist theology in networks

In the 1980s, a series of initiatives developed for the networking of feminist theology at a European level.

The European Forum for Christian Women

The roots of the 'Forum' go back to the 1960s; it was officially founded in Gwatt, Switzerland in 1982. This is a network of Christian women's organizations of all the churches in Europe, including the Roman Catholic church, and as such is a unique ecumenical organization.

'We wanted to create a forum for Christian women in Europe which would contribute towards finding a common identity, deepening Christian faith, committing oneself to the unity of the churches and human beings and thus contributing to bringing about justice and peace.'[24] This aim is a general one, relating to the church and to ecumenism, in which all those involved are women. Reference to women is not the first priority. Nevertheless, the statement goes on to say: 'We want to understand theology afresh from the standpoint of women and to devote ourselves to the theological, political and social tasks . . . We want to enable women of all age-groups to take up posts of leadership in church and society.'[25]

Feminist theological theorizing is not in the foreground of the work of the Forum, but the concrete work of women in the various churches and associations.

The European Women's Synod[26]

The idea of a women's synod goes back to the original Greek meaning of the word, a gathering of people who discuss their own interests and take decisions on them. Since the term is closely defined in most churches, there were doubts whether it was meaningful to resort to it. The decisive factor was that the expression chosen shows that women understand themselves as decision-making and that the European gathering is 'not just any gathering or conference of women'.[27]

Women's synods took place in the Netherlands in 1987, in Austria in 1992 and in Germany in 1994. All these meetings served at the same time as a preparation for the European synod announced for July 1996 in Austria. In the preparatory groups women from northern and western European countries were represented, and also from Hungary and Poland. It is the aim of this synod to make visible women's initiatives and activities, to illuminate the situation of women in Europe and to adopt standpoints, all against the background of the WCC Ecumenical Decade entitled 'Solidarity of the Church with Women', which Aruna Gnanadason describes as one of 'solidarity of women with the church'.

The synod itself is independent, but its aim is the more effective representation of the aims of women's politics and the strengthening of women in the churches.

The European Society for Theological Research by Women (ESWTR)

The ESWTR is a European network of academic theologians. It was founded in 1986 in Magliaso, Switzerland, by more than eighty women scholars. In the announcements of its foundation the following aims are mentioned:

1. To develop an academic theological association of women;
2. to further the development of feminist studies in theology;
3. to develop research proposals in dialogue.[28]

International conferences take place every two years; the most recent one was in Sweden in summer 1995. In the meantime regional groups have formed in nineteen European countries, which hold occasional regional meetings depending on the number of members. The focal points of these meetings are exchanges over current research projects.

However, specific problems also arise with the networking, which can be perhaps described as the 'contemporaneity of the uncontemporaneous'. The different cultural traditions and political changes in the East-West structure bring out differences all the more strongly. Whereas in some countries it is a matter of course that a 'women's theme' should be promoted, for others it is a tremendous step to become aware of the problems associated with the doing of theology by women. All the networks have great financial problems, since even women from the rich European countries do not have good financial support; for women from southern and eastern Europe the very participation in an international conference is often an insoluble material problem. In terms of substance the fight is constantly over the smallest common denominator.

Conclusion

Feminist theology in Europe is characterized by great differences. Beyond the discussion of what is 'feminist' about feminist theology, it is becoming clear that the very awareness of the situation of doing theology as a woman is the seedcorn of feminist theology.

Despite the differences, it has become clear that networks have the important function of strengthening those who feel isolated in their regional or church contexts. This is particularly true for the countries of southern and eastern Europe. Confessional and international networking and a link between the 'movement' and academic theology is a presupposition for its liveliness and a guarantee against ideologizing. Only this laborious work will guarantee that feminist theology continues to point towards the future.

It has proved evident that academic institutionalization is necessary:

1. It has led to the further development of feminist theology, as it creates the framework for discourse.

2. Autonomous and institutional discourse need each other. The constant challenge to feminist theology to defend and justify itself has also been able to prevent self-satisfaction; however, autonomous spheres are needed in which creative concepts or concepts in the making can be given some protection in their development.

As long as there is sexism in the churches and the academic world, living as a woman with awareness in the church or as a woman theologian means living 'on the frontier', regardless of whether this existence is understood as 'feminist' or the term is rejected. Such life can be coped with only in solidarity.

Translated by John Bowden

Notes

1. Cf. *Handbuch Feministische Theologie*, ed. Monika Maassen and Christine Schaumberger, Münster 1986, and especially the contributions by Rita Burrichter and Claudia Leuge, 14–36, and Jutta Flatters, 37–50; similarly Hedwig Meyer-Wilmes, *Rebellion auf der Grenze: Ortsbestimmung feministischer Theologie*, Freiburg 1990.

2. After the title of the book by Hedwig Meyer-Wilmes mentioned in the previous note.

3. Cf. Gabriele Kammerer, '12qm Feminismus: Vorstellung des Forschungs- und Dokumentationszentrum "Femmes et Christianisme" in Lyon', *Schlangenbrut* 12, 1994, no. 45, 42f. The experience is also confirmed by the French regional group of ESWTR.

4. Ibid.

5. Meyer Wilmes, *Rebellion auf der Grenze* (n. 1), 20.

6. Cf. *Frauenforschung oder feministische Forschung*, Beiträge zur feministische Theorie 11, 1984, and especially the contributions by Maria Mies, 7–26, 40–60.

7. Mies, ibid., 44.

8. Mies, 'Methodische Postulate zur Frauenforschung', ibid, 12.

9. Meyer Wilmes, *Rebellion auf der Grenze* (n. 1), 227.

10. Ibid., 227f.

11. Mary Daly, *Gyn/Ecology*, London 1979.

12. Cf. Monika Jakobs, 'Feministische Theologin ist kein Beruf: Von der Möglichkeit, Institutionen trotzdem mitzugestalten', *Schlangenbrut* 12, 1994, no. 44, 24f.

13. Feminist theological journals might be mentioned as an example here, *Schlangenbrut* in Germany and *Fama* in Switzerland. In addition there have been and often are autonomous projects in the sphere of education.

14. Elisabeth Gössmann, 'Abgelehnt. Geburtsfehler: weiblich', in Norbert Sommer (ed.), *Nennt uns nicht Brüder: Frauen in der Kirche durchbrechen das Schweigen*, Stuttgart 1985, 145.

15. Ibid.

16. Lucia Scherzberg, 'Kein *Nihil Obstat* für Silvia Schroer', *Schlangenbrut* 9, 1991, no. 36, 37.

17. This was the suggestion made by Helen Schüngel-Straumann in a broadcast on 'Women without Professional Chairs', by Johanna Jäger, Norddeutscher Rundfunk, 27 March 1995. She is referring to 'Der Geist, die Weisheit und die Taube', *Freiburger Zeitschrift für Philosophie und Theologie* 33, 1986, 197–225.

18. Ibid.

19. Cf. Teresa Berger, 'Vom Christusmädchen in der Krippe und der Frau am Kreuz oder: Die Historizität des Heilgeschehens und die Inkulturation des Evangeliums', *Stimmen der Zeit* 120, 1995, 251–60.

20. Andrea Blome, '". . .und theologische Frauenforschung": Schlechte Aussichte für die feministisch-theologische Professur in Münster', *Schlangenbrut* 12, 1994, nos 46, 29.

21. *Schlangenbrut* 11, 1993, no. 43; there is a reaction by Elisabeth Schüssler Fiorenza in no. 44.

22. Ibid., 30.

23. Meyer-Wilmes, *Rebellion auf der Grenze* (n. 1), 68–75.

24. *Informationsblatt des Ökumenischen Forums Christlicher Frauen in Europa*, Geneva nd.

25. Ibid.

26. Cf. *Frauen und Macht: Dokumentation der Ersten Deutschen Frauensynode*, Frankfurt am Main 1994.

27. Karin Böhmer, 'Frauensynode – Geschichte einer Bewegung', in *Frauen und Macht* (n. 26), 11.

28. *Informationen über Frauen und ihre Forschung* (a reader on the third international conference of the ESWTR), Arnoldshain 1989, 3.

'Re-Imagining' Backlash

Mary E. Hunt

Introduction

Successful backlash distorts, confuses and distracts from the progress at hand. It rewrites history and moulds the future according to its own pernicious lights. The backlash against the 4–7 November 1993 Re-imagining Conference held in Minneapolis, Minnesota, USA presents a classic case-study in this phenomenon. As a speaker at and participant in the event, I offer the following report in the hope of setting the record straight and preventing more efforts to roll back decades of feminist work in religion.

The context

It is important to locate the 'Re-imagining' controversy, as it has been dubbed by the media, in its historical context. To hear critics, one would think that suddenly and without warning previously orthodox Christian women spontaneously held a meeting at which basic theological givens were turned upside down. In truth, the conference was yet one more in a series of dozens of workshops, summer schools, graduate programmes, consultations and publishing projects which make up the rich mix that is feminist work in religion.

In the United States the movement can be traced back at least a century to the pioneering efforts of the suffrage leaders who pieced together *The Woman's Bible* as part of a strategy that linked social change with religious change. It is expressed in virtually every tradition as the 'feministization' of religions in the late twentieth century. Efforts range from the cosmetic to the structural, from language changes and the addition of women to the clergy ranks, to new forms of community and new ways of thinking about the divine. Virtually no religious assumptions have gone untouched, no presuppositions unchallenged.

'Re-imagining' was yet one more event in this history at which women scholars and activists turned their attention to strategic theologizing.[1] Like the Women-Church and Women's Ordination Conference gatherings before it, the Church Women United and Grailville meetings, the denominational women's assemblies and the annual sessions by feminist scholars at professional meetings such as the American Academy of Religion and Society of Biblical Literature, Re-imagining was one more opportunity to showcase feminist scholarship and its direct connections to the transformation of unjust, exclusive religious and social systems. To single it out as unique is to miss the significance of this larger movement of which it is a part. Indeed, to isolate it, as most critics have, is an effort to erase its antecedents and thus distort its meaning.

The Conference

The now-famous gathering of 2,300 people (mostly women but including at least 100 men) from twenty-seven countries was the North American expression of the World Council of Churches' 'Ecumenical Decade of Churches in Solidarity with Women' held at the mid-point of the Decade. It was planned by an ecumenical committee drawn from both national denominational staffs and local volunteers. Conference planning was complicated, as people from various churches and agencies ordered their priorities into a patchwork programme. They drew on an international pool of speakers and workshop leaders who represented but one small cross-section of the hundreds of feminists, womanists, mujeristas and other women in religion who bring critical perspectives to the reshaping of their respective fields.

Seed money came from some of the major denominations, notably the United Methodist and Presbyterian churches, as well as from some church women's groups. Staff time was donated by many women who took on this project as part of their professional responsibilities. But most of the financing came from the thousands of participants who paid registration fees, housing and travel costs themselves. While this was a church-related conference, it was not underwritten to any great extent by the churches, as might have been the case in other countries where taxes assure larger subsidies for such events. Rather, it was paid for by those who attended, an important point deliberately distorted by critics who would have the public think this was somehow a church-financed event hijacked by planners. Women's money, albeit with help from some churches, made it happen.

The meeting was distinguished by the sum of its creative content, as well as for its innovative liturgies, participatory plenary sessions, dynamic room arrangements, and attention to the arts, especially music. Speaker after speaker invited conference goers to 're-imagine' basic categories of theological reflection: creation, God, community, Jesus, sexuality and the family, church and ministry, language, among others. The invitation was sweetened by the encouragement of right as well as left brain activity: drawing, dancing, poetry, painting, music, silence, prayer. Common meals and shared cultural events, caucuses and exhibits combined to produce a sense that Christian feminists could create communities of struggle and celebration out of the reimagined 'compost' of their traditions.[2]

Most of the work presented was already well known to academics in the field. Controversy arose simply because in this setting it was made available to and was embraced by mainstream women, both lay and ordained, who came from and returned to local churches. By no means was there consensus on any one issue. But the common thread was a willingness to revisit, reconsider and reshape fundamental dimensions of the Christian faith tradition according to the experiences of women from different races, ethnic groups, ages, sexual orientations and denominations. Unlike some post-Christian feminist work, what distinguished Re-imagining was the claim that the results were re-imagined *Christianity*.

Participants went home with a renewed sense of empowerment as religious agents after centuries of 'kyriarchy', as well as with a renewed sense of their right and responsibility to give expression to their traditions.[3] They were buoyed by the heady experience of an international congress, and empowered by the example and enthusiasm of leaders. No wonder a vicious backlash set in almost immediately.

The backlash

Major news media in the United States gave the Re-imagining Conference scant attention as a religious event. Local press in Minneapolis was informative but not outstanding. The religious press, including such relatively progressive periodicals as *National Catholic Reporter* and *Christian Century*, included mention of it, but not the kind of extensive coverage that later attended the backlash.

Within months, a well-orchestrated campaign to discredit the event began in earnest in the secular as well as religious press. Right-wing groups linked to various denominations (i.e., not official parts of the church structures, but groups of conservative members, such as the Good News Methodists, organized on their own) published scurrilous articles about the meeting. The primary source was the on-the-scene report by Susan

Cyre, who was sent to cover the event by *The Presbyterian Layman*. Her article began: 'Destroying traditional Christian faith, adopting ancient pagan beliefs, rejecting Jesus' divinity and his atonement on the cross, creating a god(dess) in their own image, and affirming lesbian love-making were recurring conference themes.'[4] It was a caricature beyond recognition of the conference, but one which laid out what so riled opponents about the content and dynamics of the meeting. This was followed by similar attacks in other denominationally-related publications until those churches which had contributed were embroiled in internal fights over funding and jobs.[5]

Secular media, for example *The Washington Times*, carried sensationalizing articles which began to draw attention to the event long after it was over.[6] Eventually talk shows and even serious news programmes joined the fray until 're-imagining' had become a kind of code-word for all that is wrong with progressive religions.

The effort was alleged to be orchestrated by the Washington-based conservative think-tank, the Institute for Religion and Democracy. Its president, Diane Knippers, weighed in against the meeting in a *Good News* piece in which she laid out the conservative version of a religious liberty argument: 'We believe that genuine religious freedom must include the right of religious groups to define themselves and exclude those who do not share essential elements of their faith.'[7] In short, mainline denominations have every right to condemn Re-imagining since, in her view, it is not Christian. Ms Cyre, a consultant for the Institute, reiterated the argument in talk-show appearances in an attempt to present a 'reasonable' approach: women can do as they like as long as they do not use church funds and call it Christian. This unholy alliance between secular and religious groups bent on turning back the tide of the feministization of religion spells backlash.

As a result of this campaign, a number of women ministers in attendance at the meeting were subject to questioning about the orthodoxy of their beliefs when it came to hiring and promotion. Some participants reported receiving anonymous phone calls and hate mail. Mary Ann Lundy, associate for churchwide planning for the General Assembly Council of the Presbyterian Church and a key planner for the meeting, was forced to resign by pressures mounted by the right-wing. Many theologians, and notably Dr Delores S. Williams, were vilified for remarks taken out of context.[8] In all, the backlash took concrete economic forms, as denominations debated how to recoup their perceived losses for money spent on a conference in which their kyriarchal interests were thwarted.

An analysis

Backlash depends on distortions. In the case of Re-imagining, the so-called 'Sophia controversy' was created. 'Sophia' was one of many images of the divine used at the meeting. Opponents latched on to the imagery as a glitzy way to garner sympathy from those who did not understand its theological significance. The theological row about Sophia was launched to mask a power struggle between hegemonic use of masculinist language about the divine and more inclusive symbols and images found in Christian scriptures which were normative at the conference.[9] Ironically, Sophia is now a dirty word in conservative circles.

The same power struggle has been fought over myriad issues, like ordination of women and reproductive health. In the end, it is really as much over who will control theological discourse as what is said. The fact that Jesus as a male saviour figure (rather than as 'Miriam's child and Sophia's prophet', in Elisabeth Schüssler Fiorenza's helpful construction) was not central to the worship, and discussion at the meeting was twisted into cheap shots at female imagery for the divine, all aimed at discrediting the conference. Theological substance is simply passed over.

Confusion is another tool of backlash. In this instance, the on-going feminist reconstruction of the Christian faith, of which Re-imagining is a part, is obscured by undue focus on one event. Rather than grapple with the extensive feminist scholarship on the issues raised, critics isolate, personalize and exaggerate the views of those who discussed them at one meeting.

For instance, my own presentation on re-imagining sexuality included a call for responsible sexual expression in the context of loving relationships between persons who are friends. Critics, after highlighting my sexual orientation, perniciously lifted my remarks out of context to create the impression that I was calling for wholesale sex among friends. Nothing could be further from the truth. Nor was this point the essence of what I conveyed in a substantive treatment of contemporary feminist sexual ethics. Rather, the move was an effort to make the whole movement seem morally suspect and sexually promiscuous.

The net result of such strategies is to distract from the agenda at hand, something the right wing did very effectively in this case. Anti-racism remains a major challenge to feminist religious groups in this country, and one which was insufficiently addressed at the gathering. Because the backlash put organizers and participants alike on the defensive, this pressing work remains to be done. Backlash is not an excuse, but in this instance it provides a partial explanation for slow progress.

The urgency of the anti-racism work is another reason to eradicate backlash.

Likewise, dialogue with yet more scholars and activists engaged in the task of re-imagining, and concrete strategies for deepening the changes in mainline churches, beg to be accomplished. But with defensive work necessary to explain peoples' very participation in the event, such next steps are still a long way off. Happily, two subsequent Re-imagining events have been planned, and a newsletter goes to a wider Re-imagining Community, but still the backlash sets at least part of the agenda.[10]

Backlash rewrites history. Unfortunately, in the long run this conference will be known better for the controversy that followed it than for what went on during it. This means that the right wing has successfully redirected attention away from constructive work. The media co-operated implicitly. For example, many radio and television stations used uncritically a tape of cobbled excerpts from speakers and liturgies which had been crafted and distributed to reflect a reactionary point of view. Such efforts take money and know-how, both possessed by opponents of feminist work in religion, and used readily to counter the perceived threat that such moves toward equality constitute. But they also require co-operation from outside forces, in this case the media.

Such revisionist work moulds the future, as it keeps proponents so busy explaining and defending what never happened that they have little time or energy to continue the work. The toll runs high on women in the Protestant bureaucracies, who are still feeling the fall-out as their budgets are cut and their coalition work is scrutinized as never before.

The most serious impact is on those who engage in self-censorship in an effort to avoid such unpleasant and sometimes dangerous consequences in the future. This is hard to measure. But, for example, the subtle influences on committees with regard to whom to invite to speak or teach, what topics to address, and how widely to circulate so-called sensitive materials, reveal that backlash is at play.

Conclusion

The backlash against Re-imagining and all that it represents continues to be felt. It is real and dangerous for those in its wake. While its impact in this instance has been felt most directly in progressive Protestant circles, it parallels Catholic repression such as the Vatican's silencing of the Brazilian theologian Ivone Gebara. There is no reason to pretend that it does not exist, but only to acknowledge its power in an effort to stop it. Telling this story is meant to do just that.

Notes

1. See my article, 'Re-imagining: Another Fine Women's Conference', to be published in an anthology about the event edited by Pamela Carter Joern.

2. Feminist theologian Emily Culpepper coined the term 'compost' to describe her relationship to her Christian heritage in 'The Spiritual, Political Journey of a Feminist Freethinker', in *After Patriarchy: Feminist Transformations of the World Religions*, edited by Paula M. Cooey, William R. Eakin, Jay B. McDaniel, Maryknoll, NY 1991, 146–65.

3. Elisabeth Schüssler Fiorenza coined this useful word to describe 'interlocking structures of domination' in *But She Said: Feminist Practices of Biblical Interpretation*, Boston 1992, 8.

4. Susan Cyre, 'PCUSA Funds Efforts to Re-create God', *The Presbyterian Layman*, Vol. 27, No. 1, January/February 1994, 1, 4, 10–11.

5. For example, Dottie Chase, 'United Methodist Women Get Taste of Sophia Worship', *Good News*, January-February 1994, 36–8.

6. The Unification Church-related *Washington Times* carried a front page, end-of-the-year religion story about the conference on 31 December 1993.

7. Diane Knippers, 'Re-imaging Family, Liberty, and Ecumenism', *Good News*, March-April 1994, 38.

8. Delores S. Williams was widely quoted as rejecting the doctrine of the atonement. But a careful reading of her written work on the topic reveals a far more nuanced treatment. See 'Black Women's Surrogacy Experience and the Christian Notion of Redemption', in *After Patriarchy* (n. 2), 1–14.

9. See Catherine Keller, 'Inventing the Goddess', *Christian Century*, 6 April 1994, 340–2.

10. For further information on the movement and to subscribe to the quarterly newsletter write: Re-imaging Community, 122 W. Franklin Ave, Minneapolis, MN 55404 USA.

II · Different Religious Sites of Struggle

Muslim Feminist Discourses

Ghazala Anwar

I was asked to write an article exploring the range of religious and theological locations available to Muslim feminists for addressing some central issues and fundamental concerns. I would like to narrow my discussion to those Muslim feminists who have either been trained in educational institutions in Europe or North America or who have been influenced by Western intellectual traditions, even if they reside in parts of the world described as the Muslim world. I myself write as a Muslim woman born and raised in Pakistan and Saudi Arabia, who came to the United States as a student and have stayed here for educational and other reasons. I would like to acknowledge the native American soil from which I am drawing my sustenance as I reflect on Muslim feminist issues.

I define Muslim as one who surrenders to peace. I define peace as a lack of lack. Islam for me is devoid of all ugliness, injustices and oppression. It is an experience that I strive towards rather than a conglomeration of institutions, scriptures, laws, customs and rituals. I believe that such an understanding of Islam as a spiritual culture exists within my tradition. However, the locus of this spiritual culture maybe entirely elsewhere from the point understood to be the centre of the tradition. It may actually stand condemned by the official spokesmen of the tradition.

I see feminism as a movement within the general movement to restore dignity, freedom and equality not just amongst humans but amongst all who inhabit this earth. There is no conflict between my understanding of Islam, as peace, as lack of lack, and my understanding of feminism. However, there is a range of understandings as to what constitutes Islam and what constitutes feminism. Here I speak very broadly when I use the term feminist as one who makes the welfare of the lives of women a central concern of her or his life. There may not be a clear and self-evident distinction between a 'man' and a 'woman', and there are more than two sexes that belong to the human race. But for the purposes of this paper I adopt the traditional practice of categorizing each human being as either male or female, simply because this is the practice adopted by all of the people (as far as I know) who are engaged in the discussions that I seek to survey briefly in this article. However, I see that this assumption has important adverse consequences for the goal of human liberation towards which feminism seeks to work.

Contemporary feminists reflect upon various aspects of Muslim women's existence from a range of perspectives. It is not possible here to attempt a comprehensive survey of this field. I can only point out some of the salient trends within Western Muslim scholarship, writers who feel compelled to address the issue of gender-based oppression within their tradition and their communities. These feminist responses may be categorized with reference to the central authoritative texts, the Qur'an and the Hadith – and the law claimed as deriving from them. Most children born in Muslim families are taught that the Qur'an is the literal word of God and the hadith are literally the word of the Prophet Muhammad, who was divinely guided and protected from committing mistakes. Most Muslim children continue to hold these beliefs as adults. Most Muslim scholars also share in this belief. In re-negotiating gender relations, then, Muslim scholars contend with the divine authority attributed to the Qur'an and the hadith.

Muslim scholars for the most part have been hesitant (and even suspicious) of taking a historical-critical approach to the study of the Qur'an and the hadith. Yet some cautious steps in this direction have been taken. Almost four decades ago Fazlur Rahman, in his dissertation *Islamic Methodology in History*, used the historical-critical method to argue that most of the hadiths in the canonical hadith collections were spurious. His controversial work was received by Muslim scholars with reactions ranging from outright rejection to condescending tolerance. Yet it gradually steered away the modern Western-trained Muslim scholars from basing their theological arguments solely on hadith. They began to give more weight to the Qur'an than to the hadith, or even to base their arguments solely on the Qur'an. Thus even though in principle both the Qur'an and the hadith are claimed as being central and authoritative, in practice modern Western Muslim theological scholarship is centred upon the Qur'an. For Fazlur Rahman, the Qur'an was the literal word of God, and he reserved his historical critical training for the hadith literature only. Yet a similar shift on the methods used for studying the Qur'an may be imminent. Mohammed Arkoun's work on the corpus of the Qur'an is a cautious and calculated step in this direction. The Qur'an, then, enjoys far more authority than the hadith, and in this article I will confine myself to the various feminist approaches to the Qur'an only.

Central among the issues discussed by contemporary Muslim feminists are some laws that classical jurists claim to argue for on the basis of certain Qur'anic verses. Much discussed in this regard are the laws of personal status, including polygyny, physical chastisement of the wife by the husband, unilateral extra-judicial divorce by the husband, alimony, child custody, child support, inheritance, dress code and access of women to public spaces and public offices, especially that of the head of state. More recently, some communities have begun to raise the issue of liturgical leadership, particularly the leading of the Friday congregational prayers. However nowhere do I see scholars express concern for the rights of those who would live their homoerotic love for another.

One may call some of these responses 1. the apologetic; 2. the reformist; 3. the transformative; 4. the rationalist; and 5. the rejectionist. Like all categorizations this, too, is an imposition upon how things are in reality. It may help to clarify as it may also distort. Moreover the same scholar may move between the various positions listed above.

1. *The Apologists*. There are several grass roots movements associated with, inspired by, or related to, the Islamist movements in different parts of the Muslim world, which contend that Islam as preserved in the Book of God and the example of the Prophet gives the two sexes all the rights that they need for their personal well-being and fulfilment. This response makes two distinctions. First, there is an irreducible difference between the needs and wants of a man and a woman which is understood and served by the injunctions of the scriptures. Secondly, the general practice of the Muslim communities falls short of the rights given to Muslim women by the authoritative texts. Their insistence on the first, that the needs of men and women are different, might seem to most feminists a means of maintaining sexist institutions and structures. However, they also insist that the Qur'an has given women certain rights of which they are unaware; that men have taken away these rights from them or that they have given away these rights to men out of ignorance of the Qur'an. They then proceed to take back the rights given to the women by the Qur'an, and in some cases this means an improvement in the condition of the women concerned.

The basic method of studying the Qur'an used by the apologists is philological and contextual. The emphasis is not so much on trying to reinterpret the Qur'anic verses that impact on the relative status of the sexes as on educating women about their meaning and interpretations. However, more reinterpretation may actually happen in these grass-roots

Qur'anic study groups than they might be aware of. The obvious 'advantage' of this approach is that it does not threaten conservative and mainstream Muslims, and might be a 'safe' form of feminism.

2. *The Reformists*. Whereas for the Apologists the distinction between the authoritative texts and cultural practice is central, for the Reformists the distinction between the authoritative texts and its interpretations is of more significance. For the Reformists the word of God has been inadequately understood or/and misinterpreted. Like the Apologists, the Reformists, too, use philological and contextual arguments to re-interpret the Qur'anic verses, but are more conscious of the need both for re-interpretation and for their engaging in such an activity. Whereas the reformists may question the traditional interpretations, they do not question the traditional belief that the Qur'an is literally the word of God.

3. *The Transformationists*. There are some scholars who would thoroughly transform the tradition, while still remaining within the traditionally defined framework of Islamic discourse. They use classical hermeneutical strategies for creating interpretative space and for reconciling apparent contradictions and perplexities or tensions within the text. For example, a modern Indonesian scholar, Muhammad Koesnoe, uses the classical distinction between the *muhkamat* (clear, certain) verses and the *mutashabihat* (metaphorical, elusive, unclear), but in a radically different way. The verse 3.7 reads:

> He is the one who has sent down upon you the book. In it are clear (*muhkamat*) verses, those that are the mother of the book, and others that are elusive (*mutashabihat*). So as for those whose hearts are deviant, they follow the elusive ones, seeking to cause discord and seeking after esoteric meanings. But no one knows its meaning except God. Those who are firmly grounded in knowledge say 'We believe in it, all of it is from our Lord', and no one understands except those with wisdom (translation mine).

The above verse does not indicate which Qur'anic verses are *muhkamat* and which are *mutashabihat*, simply that some are *muhkamat* and some are *mutashabihat*. Traditionally, those verses of the Qur'an that seemed to have a legal import were considered to be the *muhkamat* that ought to be adhered to by the community. Koesnoe calls these same verses, considered to be legal injunctions, as the *mutashabihat*, which, if held on to, would lead the Muslims astray. In so doing he reverses an interpretative tradition of several hundred years.[1] Since 3.7 does not in fact specify which verses are *muhkamat* and which are *mutashabihat*, Muhammad Koesnoe's interpretation is as true to the text as is the other. However, the consequences of adopting his interpretation are quite far-reaching and radical. In fact they open up the possibility of entirely reconstituting Islamic law. Muhammad Koesnoe's suggestions give feminists a potent tool for dealing with all the 'sexist' verses of the Qur'an. They may all be termed *mutashabihat*, i.e. metaphorical, elusive, esoteric – dwelling or insisting upon which, as a legal or customary norm, would only mislead the Muslim community. Koesnoe makes a brilliant hermeneutical move which leaves the tradition intact while affording unlimited possibilities of transformation from within.

Similarly, the Sudanese martyr Mahmud Muhammad Taha uses another classical distinction, that between the Meccan and the Medinan verses, to present his vision of a transformed Islam. From earliest times the Qur'anic commentators sought to ascertain the place and occasion of revelation as an important context that would clarify the meaning of the verses. Taha, however, uses this distinction to assert that the Meccan Qur'an is the eternal message of Islam while the Medinan Qur'an is one possible embodiment in history of this message. The Meccan revelations are for the most part poetic, prophetic, egalitarian and visionary. The Medinan verses, on the other hand, are more prosaic. The verses that are considered to have a legislative import are Medinan. Taha's distinction again frees the interpreters of the Qur'an to re-legislate on the basis of the Meccan ethical vision. The use of this approach is self-evident to feminists. Taha himself, and one of his students Abdullahi an-Naim, have with sincerity and integrity advocated the cause of women in their writings.

Even though both Koesnoe and Taha use age-old and respected hermeneutical principles, their views have yet to be accepted, appreciated or developed by Muslim scholars or by Muslim feminists.

4. *The Rationalists*. Some feminists, like the Pakistani Riffat Hassan, assert that since God is just and compassionate, then His words can only be interpreted in terms consonant with these divine qualities.[2] This view of course imposes a criterion of justice upon the Qur'an, instead of taking what the Qur'an says as just. Or rather, it takes a vision of justice nourished by some verses of the Qur'an, and uses it to judge other verses which seem to shatter this vision of justice. I respect the ethical commitment of this position, yet it is extra-Qur'anic to the extent that it takes some verses as the standard to which the interpretation of other verses must adhere. And the decision as to which verses take primacy over others is a personal one.

There is no escape from the dilemma of reading into a text as one tries to read out of it. Yet not clearly articulating that one stands both inside and outside the Qur'anic world view, while taking a certain position on justice and equity, compromises intellectual rigour and has several disadvantages. A more serious disadvantage is that it inhibits an honest discussion of questions related to the nature of revelation (and one that is in print). What constitutes revelation? Who has the right to it? What authority does a person's claim to revelation give her or him in the larger community?

A different form of rationalism is espoused by Fazlur Rahman. He points out the need for philosophical reflection in order to come up with new theoretical frameworks for Islamic law. He laments that the early Muslim jurists' approach was fragmentary. They worked piecemeal with specific verses as the bases of specific legislation instead of deriving ethical principles from the Qur'an and making them the basis for a coherent legislation. Fazlur Rahman stresses the need for developing an Islamic theology based on the Qur'an. This theology would form the foundation for Islamic ethics, which would also be based on the Qur'an. The ethics would in turn provide the framework within which various systems of Islamic law could develop. As a rationalist and a modernist, Fazlur Rahman himself wrote articles addressing some of the legal issues of concern to women, interpreting the relevant Qur'anic verses in keeping with his liberal outlook.

5. *The Rejectionists*. There are a few Muslims who at the risk of their lives refuse to give the Qur'an the authority to discriminate against women. For them, the point of reference is the experience of women, and any argument, regardless of what its source may be, that supports the oppression of women is unacceptable. The Bangla Deshi Tasleema Nasreen is one such feminist. She has publicly stated the need to revise or reject some of the misogynist or sexist verses of the Qur'an. I have come across the opinion that she expressed publicly in private conversations amongst women. However, to take such a stand in public requires courage, given the political climate in most of the Muslim countries, and according to some Muslim women hurts the cause of the feminist movement in Muslim countries. I nevertheless support Tasleema Nasreen's action, in as far as it asserts human freedom to opt for dignity, even if it is considered to be against the will of God by most people surrounding the protagonist. The international controversy that surrounded both Rushdie's *Satanic Verses* and Tasleema's statements seems to indicate that Muslim attitudes towards the concept of revelation itself may be undergoing a transformation.

The above discussion covers some of the locations available to Muslim feminists as they reflect upon the intersection between the religion of Islam and the lives of women. In the process, they seek not only to change the social, political, economic, legal, emotional and spiritual realities for women, but also to transform the Islamic tradition itself. For no matter how intransigent or immovable the tradition might seem on certain issues, it must respond and change once enough people have the courage to ask the unasked or unaskable questions.

Bibliography

Leila Ahmad, *Women and the Advent of Islam: Historical Roots of a Modern Debate*, New Haven 1992.

Abdullahi An-Naim, *Toward an Islamic Reformation: Civil Liberties, Human Rights and International Law*, Syracuse 1990.

R. W. J. Austin, 'Islam and the Feminine', in *Islam and the Modern World*, ed. Denis MacEoin and Ahmed Al-Shahi, London 1983.

Shahla Haeri, *Law of Desire: Temporary Marriage in Shi'i Islam*, Syracuse 1989.

John Esposito, *Women in Muslim Family Law*, Syracuse 1982.

Deniz Kandiyoti (ed.), *Women, Islam and the State*, Philadelphia 1991.

Ann Elizabeth Mayer, *Islam and Human Rights: Tradition and Politics*, Boulder, Colorado 1991.

Fatima Mernissi, *Islam and Democracy: Fear of the Modern World*, New York 1992.

——, *The Veil and the Male Elite: A Feminist Interpretation of Women's Rights in Islam*, New York 1991.

——, *Doing Daily Battle: Interviews with Moroccan Women*, New Brunswick 1989.

Naila Minai, *Women in Islam: Tradition and Transition in the Middle East*, New York 1981.

Fazlur Rahman, 'Functional Interdependence of Law and Theology', in *Theology and Law in Islam*, ed. G. E. von Grunebaum, Wiesbaden 1971.

——, 'Law and Ethics in Islam', in *Ethics in Islam*, ed. Richard G. Hovannisian, Malibu, Ca 1985.

D. A. Spellberg, *Politics, Gender and the Islamic Past: The Legacy of 'Aisha bint Abi Bakr*, New York 1984.

Fedwa Malti-Douglas, *Woman's Body, Woman's Word. Gender and Discourse in Arabo-Islamic Writing*, Princeton 1991.

Judith Tucker, *Arab Women: Old Boundaries New Frontiers*, Bloomington 1993.

Bo Utas (ed.), *Women in Islamic Societies: Social Attitudes and Islamic Perspectives*, London 1988.

Charis Waddy, *Women in Muslim History*, London and New York 1980.

Wiebke Walther, *Women in Islam*, Princeton 1992.

Notes

1. This is from a conversation with Mr Koesnoe at Colordo College during 1990–1991.

2. While Riffat Hassan may also be seen as a Reformist, this was her stand in a recent speech given in March 1995 at a panel at the UN Preparatory Committee for the Fourth World Conference on Women, in New York City.

Feminist Buddhist Discourses

Chatsumarn Kabilsingh

A brief basic understanding of the nature and teaching of Buddhism is necessary, particularly for non-Buddhist readers. Buddhism is a religion which started in the sixth century BCE with a young prince of the Sakya clan in Kapilvastu, now Nepal, who was born as Prince Siddhartha. After fulfilling the primary requirements which befitted a prince, he was married to a beautiful princess and led a happy and comfortable life until he took a tour of the city and was confronted with sickness, old age and death. He was deeply troubled by the fact that human beings, once born, cannot escape this suffering. He spent time pondering how to overcome this suffering and at the age of twenty-nine left all his belongings and worldly life-style behind, to go in search of a spiritual path which would enable him to overcome the suffering of sickness, old age and death.

He spent six years wandering, testing out various methods of self-mortification as practised in those days by Indian sages, only to find that they could not answer his quest. Finally he meditated and found the answer to his quest, since then he came to be known as the Buddha – the Enlightened One.

His first sermon, given to five ascetics, was in fact the exposition of his answer to the question of human suffering. Two significant points he made before the actual sermon were, first, that he was self-enlightened, that is, that the knowledge was not handed down to him by any outside factor, and secondly, his teaching was a middle path between the two extremes of idealism and materialism.

The sermon focussed on the Four Noble Truths, namely Dukkha, Samudaya, Norodha and Marga. Dukkha is the realization that everyone born into life is subject to human suffering, i.e. sickness, old age and death. But suffering does not occur of its own accord; it is the result of something else. So there must be a cause to it, namely ignorance. This is the Second Noble Truth.

The Third Noble Truth asserts that even though there is suffering and its cause, this can be overcome. This is the cessation of suffering. The Buddha and his enlightened disciples were the living proofs of this truth.

The Fourth Noble Truth is that there is a path to end suffering. The Buddha prescribed, like a good physician, the Eightfold Path as a path to be followed by those who realize suffering and desire to be free from it.

This is the message of Buddhism in a nutshell. The Buddha spent forty-five years after his enlightenment proclaiming and making known his spiritual findings to benefit sentient beings. The teachings which followed from the first sermon may be taken as expositions of it. Later detailed explanation on different topics can be linked to the core teaching of the Four Noble Truths.

The Buddha's teaching was revolutionary in many ways. Indian culture was heavily rooted in the caste system, in which there are four major castes: priests, kings, businessmen and labourers. Each caste is inclusive, and cross-marriage between castes is not permissible. Children born of those who have transgressed this social norm sanctioned by Brahmanism are considered out-caste, much scorned by society. Only the upper castes who have access to the Vedas, the sacred texts through which one attains salvation. Amidst this social injustice, the Buddha declared the Sangha, his community, to be free from such caste distinction. To him, high or low caste depended completely on how one behaved. The caste system was rooted out from Buddhism once and for all.

Buddhism is free not only from caste difference but also from gender difference. The Buddha was hesitant to accept Queen Maha Pajapati who was his aunt and stepmother to his order, but later agreed on the basis that women are equal to men in their potential to achieve enlightenment, or spiritual salvation.

In Brahmanism, women were allowed to perform ritual only as the other half of their husbands. Women were not to study sacred texts; their only path of salvation was through unconditional faith and service to their husbands. Such social value forced women to get married, and once married they had to be able to produce a male child (if not children). It was the son who would perform the last rites for parents, to enable their souls to go to heaven. Hence women were burdened by marriage and motherhood.

In Buddhism, the Buddha removed all these burdens from women. Women can be enlightened through their own efforts. Single women and widows were treated equally in Buddhism. As a result, many women escaped from the burden of households to join the order as fully ordained nuns. Monks and nuns in early Buddhism were treated equally by the Buddha.

In the beginning they shared the same set of monastic rules, but as time passed by more rules grew as the community became larger. Some of the rules were added exclusively for the monks and some others exclusively for the nuns, and some are applicable to both. Interestingly, certain rules were laid down for the monks to follow so that they would not exploit the nuns. Study of the development of monastic rules clearly shows that the Buddha took the role of a father to make sure that the nuns, his younger daughters, would not be taken advantage of by their older brothers, the monks.

Some of the nuns were highly praised by the Buddha as being foremost in preaching, in strictness of observing monastic rules, etc. The nuns shared equal responsibility as propagators of Buddhism. Some of them came from royal families. Khema was the queen of King Bimbisara before she joined the order, not to mention Queen Pajapati, the first nun, who was the Buddha's aunt and stepmother. Hundreds of them were enlightened. They were the true light for Buddhists of later periods.

However, only three months after the passing away of the Buddha, the first Council was held. 500 enlightened monks were invited to it, and no nuns. Eight charges were laid against Ananda, the Buddha's cousin and attendant. One of them was that Ananda was responsible for having nuns included in the order.

As time passed, many values suppressing and rejecting women crept back into the order, drawn from Indian society. It is not surprising, therefore, to find passages in the Buddhist canonical texts referring to women as inferior.

Interesting work has been done by feminist scholars on the Tripitaka (Buddhist canonical texts) to sift the spirit or essence of Buddhism, which is generally liberating for women, from negative social values which derived mainly from Brahmanism.

Anyone who reads the Tripitaka without this awareness can easily fall into the trap of thinking that Buddhism is biassed against women, that Buddhism is patriarchy and responsible for many social ills of which women have been victims.

Ordination of women was granted by the Buddha, yet at present Buddhist women in many Buddhist countries like Thailand, Sri Lanka, Myanmar, etc., do not have the privilege of continuing the lineage. Technically, the ordination of women must be dual, first by the community of nuns (a minimum of five) and then by a monastic community of the same number. Countries where nuns never existed technically cannot start the order of nuns.

However, in the third century BCE Sanghamitta and a group of nuns went to Sri Lanka at royal request and gave ordination to hundreds of women. Later Sri Lankan nuns went to China and established the nuns' order in China. This order of nuns spread to neighbouring countries. When Buddhism spread to the West, women among the new Buddhists started asking for ordination. In 1988 at Hsi Lai Temple in Los Angeles 200 nuns (with lower ordination) from various Buddhist traditions received full ordination. This ordination lineage continues up to the present.

Ordination of women is one of the major concerns among Buddhist women internationally. The World Council of Churches is aware of problems of the same nature which women face in various religions. Sponsorship has been provided so that women can share and learn from each other.

Buddhist women in Asian countries are traditionally conservative and submissive. This is understandable, as in some countries Buddhism has been the exclusive domain of monks. Women participate only at the level of making offerings, and giving support to the temples and to the monks.

With the introduction of feminism, Buddhist women are strengthened. Feminist Buddhists are learning to find strength in going back to the texts as a source of authority. They find subtle strength in putting Dharma (the teaching) into practice, so they are well balanced spiritually. With this new strength Buddhist women can march into the future as full partners, equally responsible for the growth or decline of Buddhism. This responsibility was given to them by the Buddha himself.

For Further Reading

Tsultrim Allione, *Women of Wisdom*, London 1984.
Sandy Boucher, *Turning the Wheel. American Women Creating the New Buddhism*, Boston 1993.
Rita Gross, 'Buddhism after Patriarchy?', in *After Patriarchy. Feminist Transformations of the Religions*, ed. P. M. Cooey, W. R. Eakin and Jay B. McDaniel, Maryknoll 1991, 65–86.
Hanna Havenik, *Tibetan Buddhist Nuns: History, Cultural Norms, Social Reality*, Oslo nd.
Anne Carolyn Klein, *Meeting the Great Bliss Queen. Buddhists, Feminists and the Art of the Self*, Boston 1995.
Karma Lekshe Tsomo, *Sakyadhita: Daughters of the Buddha*, Ithaca, NY 1988.

Jewish Feminist Theological Discourses

Adele Reinhartz

Jewish feminist discourses range over many issues, some of which are common to the Jewish community as a whole, and others of which are specific to particular geographical, political and social contexts. In keeping with the theme of this issue of *Concilium*, this survey will focus on Jewish feminist attempts to 'image' divinity. Two principal questions will be addressed. What are appropriate liturgical expressions for feminist God-images? What are the implications of these expressions for Jewish feminist theology and community? Although these questions are broadly relevant, the survey will centre on the work of Jewish feminists who share certain cultural similarities (North American, white, Ashkenazi [of Eastern European origin], Jewishly educated, middle-class), though not sexual orientation or denominational affiliation.

The starting point for Jewish feminist God-imaging is the recognition of the profound patriarchy of traditional Jewish God-language. Classical Jewish theology recognizes that God-language is metaphorical; God is neither male nor female. Nevertheless, masculine God-language is deeply and firmly embedded in traditional liturgy and theology; the occasional use of female imagery does not detract from this in any significant way. Inherent in this male imagery are the concepts of domination and hierarchy which mirror male social roles. These images function as 'models of and models for', claiming to describe the divine nature, while in fact legitimating a human community that reserves power and authority for men.[1]

The task of Jewish feminist theology is therefore to transform the metaphors for God that have informed the Jewish imagination and shaped Jewish self-understanding and behaviour.[2] Approaches to this task fall into two categories: reinterpretation of traditional imagery, and revisioning of God-language.

I Feminist reinterpretation

Though Jewish feminists dissent from the patriarchal emphasis of the traditional liturgy, they may nevertheless value the connection which that liturgy provides to the broader Jewish community in space and time. Feminist reinterpretation of patriarchal language allows for the retention of at least some of the traditional divine epithets while imbuing them with a content that is more consistent with a feminist theology.

Rabbi Lynn Gottlieb has experimented at some length with this approach. Her reinterpretations of traditional God-images, based on a creative exploration of their Hebrew meanings and/or the Hebrew letters of which they are composed, infuses them with a vivid feminist spirituality. *Elohim* is not God but 'all spirits'; *Adonai* is not Lord but the 'I as the ground of experience', and 'the door to the mystery of life'; *Shaddai* becomes 'my breasts' and *Shekhinah*, 'She who dwells within'.[3]

Another candidate for feminist reinterpretation is the epithet *HaMakom* (literally 'the place'). This spatial term may be used to express the sense of community as the space within which God's activity is made known and acknowledged.[4] Even the tradiitional male image of God as father might find its place in the context of a re-imaged feminist Judaism, not as a paternalistic image of hierarchy and domination, but simply as a parental image.[5]

II Feminist revisioning

Most effort, however, has been directed towards the creative use of Jewish tradition and the Hebrew language to give theological and liturgical expression to Jewish feminist 'God-wrestling'.[6]

1. Feminine God titles

One way of creating feminist God-language is to replace masculine personal pronouns and images with feminine ones, while retaining the traditional structure of blessings and other liturgical formulae. The ubiquitous title *ha-kadosh barukh hu* ('the Holy One, Blessed be He') is feminized by adding the feminine ending to Hebrew for 'Holy One' and replacing the masculine pronoun with the feminine. Similarly, the familiar image of God as 'King of the Universe' can become 'Queen of the Universe' by adding the feminine ending to the Hebrew word for king. This simple solution, however, is often considered inadequate. Replacing the masculine images with feminine equivalents does not erase the images of domination, which are seen as inappropriate in a feminist liturgy.[7]

A second approach is to utilize the Hebrew words for goddess: *Elohut* (a feminine noun meaning divinity), and *Elah* (meaning Goddess).[8] Though goddess language may have polytheistic connotations for some,[9] others argue that reimaging the Goddess through the lens of Jewish monotheism may enrich the range of metaphors for addressing God.[10]

The most popular female God-image is *Shekhinah*, frequently incorporated into a feminized blessing formula, 'Blessed be the *Shekhinah*'.[11] Although the term appears in a variety of contexts in rabbinic literature, it is not until the thirteenth century Kabbalistic (mystical) text that it is used to represent the feminine element in God.[12] In the Zohar, the *Shekhinah* is identified with the tenth *Sefira* (divine emanation), which must be united with the Godhead in order for salvation to occur. This union is depicted in explicitly sexual terms; indeed, 'every true marriage is a symbolical realization of the union of God and the Shekhinah'.[13]

The attractiveness of this term lies in the explicitly feminine language in which it is described. Identified with the community of Israel, *Shekhinah* represents 'the mystical idea of Israel in its bond with God and in its bliss, but also in its suffering and its exile. She is not only Queen, daughter and bride of God, but also the mother of every individual in Israel.'[14] On the other hand, the concept of sexual union between the *Shekhinah* and the rest of the *Sefiroth* reinforces the image of God as masculine and limits the notion of the feminine to sexuality.[15] For this reason, some feminist theologians argue that *Shekhinah*, though a feminine term, can be useful only if at least partly wrenched free from its original context and radically reinterpreted.[16]

2. *Images of mutuality*

The feminine God-titles maintain the classical covenantal notion of a hierarchical relationship between God and Israel. In sharp contrast are images of God as lover, friend, companion and co-creator which impute mutuality and partnership to this bond. In English these labels are not gender-specific and may denote either male or female, while in Hebrew they may be translated as either masculine or feminine. Such images emerge from traditional Jewish sources, though they may be found outside those sources as well.[17] The feminist understanding of God as lover, for example, is taken not from Hosea, which maintains the patriarchal relationship between God as male lover and Israel as errant but beloved woman, but from the Song of Songs, which presents male and female as pursuer and pursued.[18] The idea of God as friend is present in the Yom Kippur (Day of Atonement) liturgy, providing a symbol of mutuality in the covenantal relationship between God and Israel. The image of

companion, while lacking the exclusiveness of friendship, implies a sense
of equality and community, shared goals and shared work. Similarly,
epithets prefixed with 'co-', as in 'co-creator', imply the notion of
partnership between divinity and humanity in 'the larger project of world-
creation', emphasize communal endeavours, and conjure up 'a sense of
personal empowerment and mutual responsibility'.[19]

Because these images, while personal, are applicable to both male and
female, they resist the restriction of particular attributes to either male or
female aspects of God. The human community that exists in the image of
such a God is a collective of women and men whose social roles and
relationships are not dictated by their gender. In imputing mutuality to the
God-human relationship, such images emphasize human responsibility.
Erasing the notion of hierarchy, however, requires radical rethinking of
foundational Jewish symbols such as the Exodus, which has traditionally
been seen as the confirmation of God's caring action on behalf of Israel as
God's people. Furthermore, images of mutuality do not give expression to
the range of negative emotion and experience, including the feelings of
powerlessness in the face of misfortune and tragedy, which often act as a
stimulus for prayer.

3. Non-personal God-language

Non-personal God-language has been explored most extensively by
Marcia Falk, in her reworking of traditional blessings. Falk does not
simply substitute a different set of imagery for the masculine language of
the formula, nor does she create a set formula of her own to introduce each
blessing. Rather, she considers the spiritual significance of the blessing and
then reformulates it in such a way as to reflect that meaning. For example,
the traditional blessing to be recited on special occasions (such as wearing
new clothes or eating a new type of fruit) is as follows: 'Blessed are you, O
Lord, King of the universe, who revives us, sustains us and brings us to
this time.' Falk's version reads: 'Let us bless the flow of life [*ma'ayan
hahayyim*] that revives us, sustains us, and brings us to this time.'[20]

Falk has changed two important parts of the blessing. The initial
change, which substitutes 'Let us bless' for 'Blessed are you', shifts one's
attention from the one being blessed to the individuals/community
invoking the blessing. Second, the divine epithet 'flow of life' is both non-
personal and non-hierarchical. Falk's rendering of the blessing evokes the
passage of time as well as the special moments in time for which the
blessing expresses thanks.

In her blessing for the sanctification of wine at Sabbath and festival
meals, Falk departs further from the traditional form while still maintain-

ing its sense of rhythm and some of its vocabulary. The traditional form reads: 'Blessed are you, O Lord, King of the universe, creator of [or: who creates] the fruit of the vine.' Falk's version reads: 'Let us bless the source of life [*eyn hahayyim*] that nurtures fruit on the vine as we weave the branches of our lives into the tradition.'[21] The term 'source of life', a non-personal feminine term in Hebrew, evokes the nurturing and sustaining of life rather than the creation of life from nothingness implied in the traditional term 'creator'. Rather than simply expressing thanks for the Sabbath wine, the blessing articulates the meaning of the act of sanctification for the individuals and community invoking the tradition.

Falk's blessings counter the image of God as a personal power that stands above, outside, or even alongside creation. Instead, the divine is envisaged as the force within creation from which the world and its inhabitants draw their sustenance and creative power. Human beings are transformed from passive recipients of God's largesse to active participants in the creative process and in the divine-human relationship itself. The epithets 'source of life' and 'flow of life' imply that human beings created in the image of God are similarly participating in the creative cycle of nature as well as in the creation of community through the distinctly Jewish practices which many of the blessings accompany. Submerged in this approach to God-talk, however, is the notion of a personal God, a Being to whom one might cry out, in gladness and in pain, in gratitude and in anger. The shift from the personal to the non-personal God similarly has implications for the conception of the historical relationships among the individual, the community of Israel and the divine.

III Liturgy, theology and community

The above discussion demonstrates the diversity of Jewish feminist theological discourses. None of these options is satisfying and complete in itself, nor, in fact, is it intended to be. Rather, feminist God-formulations are not understood as mutually exclusive, but complementary; not definitive, but simply directions 'towards' a feminist theology.[22] Though individual theologians may have their own preferences, diversity is valued as a source of strength, not feared as a threat to the whole.

In addition to the value of diversity, several other points emerge. First, a primary concern of Jewish feminist theological discourse is not simply to talk *about* God but to name and re-name the divinity. One reason for this concern is the connection between God-talk and liturgy, to which divine epithets are more suited than abstract theological discourse. Theology is therefore important not only for its own sake but also as a preparation for the transformation of liturgy and as an undergirding for the reformation of the praxis of communal prayer.

Second, Jewish feminist discourses exhibit the tension between universality and particularity that is inherent in Jewish sources and Jewish thought as a whole. Feminist discourse, however, has been more successful in depicting the universality of humanity than the particularity of the Jewish experience thereof. Although Jewish feminist God-names and the ritual contexts in which they are used are drawn from Jewish tradition, the divine-human bond which they imply is frequently grounded not in the particularity of Jewish history but in universal human experience. Yet the creative tension can be maintained only if the particularity of Jewish experience is also given theological expression. The hierarchical language traditionally used for describing the Exodus, Sinai and the covenantal relationship between God and Israel needs to be reformulated in a way which gives expression to a feminist consciousness without submerging or erasing these pivotal experiences.

Equally important, and equally problematic, is the relationship between *halakhah* (Jewish law) and theology. *Halakhah* is traditionally seen as the expression of the divine will for the Jewish people. Yet *halakhah* not only contains specific laws which limit women's social and religious roles and activities but also embodies a view of women as fundamentally 'Other'. Can *halakhah* be transformed so as to allow for the retention of a distinctively Jewish identity while at the same time eliminating its patriarchal and androcentric world-view?

The problem of *halakhah* looms large in the arena of communal prayer. In Orthodox Judaism, women are not counted in the prayer quorum, nor are they allowed access to religious leadership roles.[23] The specific laws in which this exclusion is grounded have been the subject of considerable halakhic discourse on the part of both men and women.[24] But feminist theologians argue strongly that one cannot achieve full equality for women by isolating and 'fixing' particular *halakhot*. Rather, the halakhic system as a whole, its theological basis and its liturgical expression must be subjected to feminist critique. Such critique fosters attempts to incorporate feminist God-language and women's experience into the content and structure of Jewish communal prayer.

Departing from the fixed liturgy in these respects, however, raises a new challenge: how can communal prayer, which presupposes at least a measure of uniformity in content and structure, give expression to the individuality of women's experience and the diversity of Jewish feminist God-naming? One community that has taken up this challenge is B'not Esh, a group of women that has been meeting annually since 1981 and has developed a model for building sustained community across considerable geographic distance.[25] Martha Ackelsberg, a charter member of B'not Esh, has detailed their efforts to develop a model for communal prayer that also respects individual experience. Because no one form could possibly satisfy everyone, these efforts 'generated high levels of frustration and anger'.[26] Nevertheless, the process of working through these expectations over time, and experimenting with different forms, resulted in the development of a liturgy which permitted group prayer.[27]

The creating of feminist liturgy and community is a never-ending process. Jewish feminist theological discourses will continue God-wrestling, not only by further development of feminist God-images but also by confronting a range of related questions, such as the nature of evil, the meaning of covenant, the impact of feminist micro-communities on the larger Jewish community, and education and access of feminists to leadership roles in Jewish communal and religious institutions. Such attempts will no doubt be characterized by continued creativity and a positive evaluation of human diversity within the context of strong commitment to Jewish feminist spirituality and transformation.

Notes

1. Judith Plaskow, *Standing Again at Sinai: Judaism from a Feminist Perspective*, San Francisco 1990, 123, 127.
2. Ibid., 121.
3. Ellen Umansky, 'Creating a Jewish Feminist Theology', in *Weaving the Visions: New Patterns in Feminist Spirituality*, ed. Judith Plaskow and Carol P. Christ, San Francisco 1989, 192–3.
4. Plaskow, *Standing Again* (n. 1), 141–2.
5. Ibid., 166.
6. Ibid., 33.
7. Marcia Falk, 'Notes on Composing New Blessings', in *Weaving the Visions* (n. 3), 129.
8. Neither is biblical, however. The former is found in rabbinic literature (e.g. Genesis Rabbah, ch. 46), while the latter is found in modern Hebrew dictionaries.
9. Umansky, 'Theology' (n. 3), 192.
10. Plaskow, *Standing Again* (n. 1), 152.
11. Annette Daum, 'Language and Liturgy', in *Daughters of the King: Women and the Synagogue*, ed. Susan Grossman and Rivka Haut, Philadelphia 1992, 187.
12. Gershom G. Scholem, *Major Trends in Jewish Mysticism*, New York 1941, 229.
13. Ibid., 235.
14. Ibid., 230.
15. Daum, 'Language' (n. 11), 187; cf. Falk, 'Blessings', 192–30.
16. Plaskow, *Standing Again* (n. 1), 139–40; cf. Daum, 'Language' (n. 11), 200.

17. The images of God as friend and lover, for example, are developed by Sallie McFague, *Metaphorical Theology: Models of God in Religious Language*, Philadelphia 1982, 177–92.

18. Plaskow, *Standing Again* (n. 1), 162.

19. Ibid., 163.

20. Ellen Umansky and Dale Ashton (eds.), *Four Centuries of Jewish Women's Spirituality: A Source Book*, Boston 1992, 242.

21. Ibid.

22. Judith Plaskow, 'The Coming of Lilith: Toward a Feminist Theology', in *Womanspirit Rising: A Feminist Reader in Religion*, ed. Carol P. Christ and Judith Plaskow, San Francisco 1979, 198–209; Rita Gross, 'Steps Toward Feminine Imagery of Deity in Jewish Theology', in *On Being a Jewish Feminist*, ed. Susannah Heschel, New York 1983, 234–47.

23. Non-Orthodox Jewish denominations as well as many non-denominational groups have addressed this problem to varying degrees. For the history of the process within Conservative Judaism see Neil Gillman, *Conservative Judaism: The New Century*, New Jersey 1993, 124–49.

24. Contrast, for example, the Orthodox views of Moshe Meiselman, *Jewish Woman in Jewish Law*, New York 1978, 43–57, and the feminist perspective of Rachel Biale, *Women and Jewish Law*, New York 1984, 10–43.

25. Martha A. Ackelsberg, 'Spirituality, Community and Politics: B'Not Esh and the Feminist Reconstruction of Judaism', *Journal of Feminist Studies in Religion* 2, 1986, 118.

26. Ibid.

27. Ibid., 113.

A Church in Solidarity with Women: Utopia or Symbol of Faithfulness?

Aruna Gnanadason

'Every time I beat my wife she must thank me, because she is one step closer to salvation!' said a church leader in the Cook Islands, when confronted with the fact that there is domestic violence even in the families of clergy and others in leadership.

'It is my cultural right to beat my wife', claimed a student of theology in India.

'I am tired, very tired of always having to react to the actions of the management', said the only woman who is tenured to teach in a theological college in the USA.

In Zimbabwe, in a library of a theological college which does not yet admit women students, in the section on 'Pastoral Care', tucked away between titles such as *God is For the Alcoholic* and *The Funeral*, one finds a few books on feminist theology, which have obviously not been referred to even once!

An event that provoked a lot of controversy in recent times was the Reimagining Conference – a gathering held in Minneapolis in November 1993, in the context of the Ecumenical Decade of the Churches in Solidarity with Women. The more than 2000 women and a few men gathered there claimed their space and their right to reimagine community, the earth, ministry, traditional church doctrines, Jesus and God – from the context of women's life experiences in an unjust, patriarchal world. In faith and faithfulness, the women had reflected on what it means to be Christian women today, only to be branded as 'heretical' by ultra-conservative interest groups within several denominations. To the women who had participated in the event the negative reactions that it provoked were both unexpected and very unjust – their 'safe space' had been invaded.

At the heart of all these reactions and attitudes lies 'a theological problem'. The church has been unable to acknowledge the patriarchal violence that has existed and continues to exist in our societies. Christianity, like other religions, has in fact given theological legitimation for the violence and has therefore sanctioned it.

But then, the ray of hope that shines through these harsh realities is the fact that women have begun speaking out. They have sought their spaces and claimed their right to seek a paradigm shift in theology. Women demand justice and a violence-free world, in which they can participate creatively, on their own terms.

It was in such a context, when women had already emerged as an organized force in church and society, that the World Council of Churches' Ecumenical Decade of the Churches in Solidarity with Women was launched by the churches world-wide in 1988. The seed for a Decade of the Churches in Solidarity with Women was planted with the announcement of the UN Decade for Women (1975–1985). The Central Committee of the World Council of Churches (WCC), at its meeting in 1985, when listening to a report on the achievements of the UN Decade, decided that there was a need for the churches to ensure some kind of continuity to the UN process. Such a commitment took more concrete shape when in its meeting in 1987, the Central Committee decided to observe a Decade of the Churches for solidarity action with women – it was seen as a *kairos* moment for the churches to act. It was not accidental that the Advisory Working Group on Women of the WCC, at its meeting in Mahabalipuram in India, proposed that the Easter message be the Leitmotif for the launch of the Decade during the Easter season of 1988. The focus was on the question the women ask each other, as they walk towards the tomb: 'Who will roll the stone away?'

Mercy Oduyoye, the Ghanaian theologian, then Deputy General of WCC, wrote:

The imagery of stones as stumbling blocks hampering women's lives was a fertile ground for discussion. The stream of 'resurrection people' that has flowed from the empty tomb has continued to broaden and deepen. The story of the two who walked with the risen Christ towards Emmaus without recognizing him was also helpful as we planned for a journey that would take ten years to complete. Each step counts and each move has to be checked with the risen Christ. On this journey we shall constantly be in conversation with Christ who will help us to interpret the past record of the church in relation to women.[1]

There is no doubt that there was a spurt of enthusiasm when the Decade was launched, and many plans were made to act in solidarity with women. Mercy Oduyoye describes succinctly what has been done in different regions during the first years of the Decade, in the booklet *Who Will Roll the Stone Away?*, quoted from earlier. There are reports in the book of some vivid demonstrations of solidarity actions by churches around the world – these have to be acknowledged.

But what is more significant is that particularly the women of the churches have grasped the moment to articulate some of their deepest aspirations and longings in an attempt to ensure responsive action on the part of the churches. This is one of the most obvious gains of the Decade – the opportunity it has provided for women to come together to enunciate their visions and hopes for a better world. Women have begun recognizing the commonality of their struggles and are reaching out to each other beyond all humanly made boundaries. The global nature of their struggles has been vividly demonstrated in the course of this Decade.

The purpose

The purposes of the Ecumenical Decade are wide enough to encourage all concerns that women are working on locally, nationally, regionally and globally. As one hears of issues from around the world that women are dealing with, one is struck by the amazing commonality of concerns, though there are no doubt specificities, depending on the context. It is after all the same patriarchal structures in church and society that keep women 'in place' all over the world!

Stones that are stumbling blocks

An Easter Message was sent out to the churches, with an invitation to the churches to participate in the launch of the Decade. The Message pointed to the stones that could hamper the journey:

> There are practices and teachings in the churches that are obstacles to women's creative theological spiritual and decision-making contribution in church and society. There are structures and patterns of leadership and ministry that block partnership between women and men . . . [2]

The Decade has focussed on *empowering women*, so that women can be the ones to determine the agenda of concerns that the churches will act on. It is up to women to decide what structures need to be challenged in their church, their country, their region and in the world. However, this is the Churches' Decade, and *not* a women's decade, which makes it clear that structural changes can come about only when the whole community of women and men in the *church will act in solidarity with women*. For this to be realized, it becomes imperative for the churches to affirm the leadership and the decisive contributions women can make to the decision-making tasks and the theological and spiritual life of the church. This implies that the time is *now* for the churches carefully to evaluate their patterns of administration and ministry to make them more inclusive of the gifts and talents women yearn to bring into the life of the church.

There is no question that the Decade came at a crucial moment in church history. It is a time when women are ready to articulate ways by which the church can crystallize into action some of its commitments to women. It is a time when women have felt empowered to speak out boldly their visions and hopes for the future of the church and the world. It is a time when women feel able to move away from being victims of oppression into a discovery of their power to reclaim their dignity and determine their destiny. It is a time when women have been able to express in many creative ways their faith and hope in a new community, a new church.

It is a time when feminist discourse is emerging all over the world. New feminist paradigms in theology, in spirituality as also in societal change, in patterns of family life and in new forms of human relationships, are now becoming spoken of by women all over the globe. These voices are no longer merely a reform movement in the church and society, they call for radical newness. They are voices sharing a warning but also of hope, urging that unless there is a readiness to move away from the familiar, the beaten path into a new way of asking questions and finding answers – there is no future. They are voices of challenge to all forms of violence and oppression that have overwhelmed the church and society. It is these voices that can transform the church into a sign and symbol of a new community in Christ.

The theological perspective that has been brought alive by women must be taken more seriously by the church. Theology from the perspective of women in struggle – the feminist theologies which have emerged all over the world – has very crucial and important insights to convey. This unfortunately is often undermined, denying the church an avenue of rich contribution. The language of liturgy and the language for naming God have been seriously restricted, excluding the experiences of women.

The key to the cry for greater participation, therefore, is *not* just a demand for a few more token women representatives in committees, etc., it is not merely a question of encouraging a few more women into ordained ministry, nor is it a demand for just a few more resolutions and statements of support – the cry is for more. It is for more inclusiveness; it is a cry for genuine partnership between women and men; it is a cry for faithfulness to the new community promised in Christ. It is a cry for the church to be truly in solidarity with women.

More stones that stand in the way of building community

The Easter Message that heralded the launch of the Decade pointed out that this solidarity with women cannot be restricted to a few structural or ecclesiological changes within the life of the church – important as these changes are – because the church around the world is placed in a societal context, which seriously threatens any semblance of community. The Message described it this way:

> In most instances women experience the worst effects of poverty, economic injustice, racism, casteism, militarism, and in denial of land and minority rights . . . Women's bodies are abused by medical technology and sold into prostitution. Women are victims of various forms of violence . . . We as church are not free from idolatries and power structures that oppress people. We do not admit that we sin by creating and justifying obstacles that destroy God's purposes for the earth. We do not empower women to challenge oppressive structures in the global community, our country and our church.[3]

We live in a context where death-dealing forces are rampant which have a particularly deleterious effect in the lives of women. A new community cannot be realized in a context where women face such institutionalized and blatant expressions of violence in the dailiness of their lives. As I write this I have before my mind's eye the life of the Filipino domestic worker, Flor Contemplacion, who was executed in Singapore a few weeks ago for a crime she did not commit. The life of migrant women workers around the world is closely interwoven with systems of exploitation and injustice – making them vulnerable to all kinds of abuse. The fact that they are most often an unorganized part of the work-force makes them susceptible to violence. Flor Contemplacion is but a symbol of the violence with which millions of women live. Her story demonstrates that the violence that women experience is rooted in unjust economic structures which thrive on the labour and sexuality of the world's powerless – particularly the women of the world. Her story is one more evidence of the racism that thrives in our world, and the fact that women under racism are primary victims of economic violence.

Therefore it is indeed appropriate that as women from the regions identified the issues they would concentrate attention on in the remaining years of the Decade, they decided on these three: violence against women both in church and society; economic injustice and its impact on women globally; and the effects of racism and xenophobia on women.

But then we do move into the last part of the Decade with many questions unanswered and unresolved. What does solidarity mean in a context which has so systematically denied women their life and creativity? That is the issue that confronts us as we approach the end of the Decade. Many negative attitudes to women and practices and doctrines that discriminate against women have not changed at all since the Decade was launched. What we also see is that in many circles it is becoming 'politically correct' to speak about women, or to initiate programmes for women: what does solidarity mean in this context, where women and their rights and struggles are being appropriated and sometimes women feel co-opted, by the churches, by governments and by their communities. What does solidarity mean in a context where in fact women see an increase in the violence – a backlash – because of their organized strength? What does solidarity mean within the ecumenical movement, which often overlooks the need for mutual accountability and challenge among member churches on ethical issues such as those relating to the life and participation of women?

If we look to the past nearly fifty years since the formation of the World Council of Churches, there is enough evidence to say that WCC *as a council* has attempted to respond with faithfulness to the visions and aspirations of women. Such expressions of solidarity have been expressed since the first Assembly of the World Council of Churches in Amsterdam, in the year 1948. But, as Mercy Oduyoye warns:

> Within the membership of WCC, solidarity with women is a tenuous factor. Recommendations painfully and painstakingly made on this issue seem to apply only to the churches-in-council and not to the individual member churches. Solidarity with women means different things for different churches . . . Sometimes one is inclined to wonder whether the churches are in solidarity with the Council on this issue. Agreements on principle do not match the practices of several member churches, and often one is inclined to conclude that the Council and its members are not of one mind.[4]

Then where do we go from here? At the end of the Decade will we be able to celebrate a church in solidarity with women? That is the question hovering over us. The Easter Message called for repentance. Are the churches ready for that? This has been a long debate, as different groups of women have tried to assess what the end of the Decade means to the churches and how it can be marked and remembered. Will it be an occasion for celebration or will it be a time of mourning? Perhaps what is needed is pragmatism – ten years that have constituted the Ecumenical Decade, or even the fifty years since the formation of WCC into a Council, are but a drop within the context of 2000 years of patriarchal history!

'The Ecumenical Decade of the Churches in Solidarity with Women is a gift from God to the churches. It is now up to the churches to nurture it and see it grow, bear fruit and have strong branches and firm roots.' That was the wishful thinking of an Indian woman when we were discussing our hopes and aspirations for this Decade, at the time of its launch. Her words express the deep longing of women the world over, to see the churches crystallize into concrete action some of the commitments they have made to women for many years now. The churches by their very nature should uphold the humanity of women, if they are to be faithful to the liberation promise offered to all in Jesus Christ. Therefore, the demand of women for a new community in Christ is *not* an unrealistic or utopian vision; it is a demand for faithfulness. It is something that must become possible and real if the church is to be the church of Jesus Christ.

Notes

1. Mercy Oduyoye, *Who Will Roll the Stone Away?*, Geneva 1990, 1–2.
2. Easter Message for the launch of the Decade, Easter Season 1988, *Decade Link* 1, February 1988.
3. Ibid.
4. Oduyoye, *Who Will Roll the Stone?* (n. 1), 44–5.

Praxis versus Image: Women towards Priesthood in the Roman Catholic Church

Jacqueline Field-Bibb

The Second Vatican Council challenged the self-identity of the Roman Catholic Church that had developed over the centuries. *Aggiornamento* rooted the church in contemporary social structures and implicitly challenged its ahistorical image. Among the issues that emerged, albeit peripherally, was that of women as priests. This article looks at the raising of the question and the defensive position of this church a decade later *vis à vis* the Church of England's momentum on the issue. Although the icon imagery that is defended is essential to a pre-Vatican II self-image of the church, the crucial question is whether this self-image is rooted in Christian origins.

Vatican II arguably cleared the way for Roman Catholic women to request ordination. The emphasis on the people of God, on community, on developing the talents of all were apparent.

> Every type of discrimination, whether social or cultural, whether based on sex, race, colour, social condition, language, or religion, is to be overcome and eradicated as contrary to God's intent. For in truth it must still be regretted that fundamental personal rights are not yet being universally honoured. Such is the case of a woman who is denied the right and freedom to choose a husband, *to embrace a state of life*, or to acquire an education or cultural benefits equal to those recognized for men [italics added] (*Gaudium et Spes* 29).[1]

This flashed on to the metaphorical hoardings. Yet did the Council utter a misleading prompt or at least an unrealistic invitation? The cue nevertheless was promptly taken up by women. Many theologians began to argue in support. Yet can argument win against a non-democratic institution, an institution moreover where Opus Dei has powerful canon lawyers in key Vatican posts? Is all we can expect realistically a repetition of early church history, namely a split between those following in the footsteps of some Johannine communities pursuing truth and relationships on the one hand and those opting for an institutional church as an authority on the other?

Between the momentum derived from the Council (1962–65) and the attempted emergency stop that was the Declaration (1976),[2] a number of books appeared on the subject. Of the first were Mary Daly's *The Church and the Second Sex* (1968)[3] and Vincent Emmanuel Hannon's *The Question of Women and the Priesthood* (1967).[4] Daly attended a session of the Council on a borrowed press pass. Her perception of the scene was akin to a Fellini film, the active red-robed cardinals contrasting starkly with the small group of self-deprecating female auditors in long black dresses and veils, and this experience determined the perspective of her already commissioned book. She highlighted the anti-feminism in church history, tradition and practice. In her examination of the priesthood issue she refuted biblical, traditional and symbolic arguments and quoted from Pope John XXIII's *Pacem in Terris*:

> Human beings have the right to choose freely the state of life which they prefer, and therefore the right to establish a family, with equal rights and duties for men and women, and also the right to follow a vocation to the priesthood or the religious life.[5]

She warned against two extreme reactions, namely of those who see the issue as premature and of those who see the ordination of women as the panacea of all ills. Hannon's book meanwhile was ground-breaking in that it raised a virtually taboo question. Written in more guarded terms than Daly's, it did not produce quite the same reaction. Whereas Hannon remained a member of her religious order, Daly was fired from her teaching post, subsequently reinstated following nationwide protests, and then left the church. Daly raised and is still raising profound questions which must be addressed by those who expect to see women as priests. As will be argued below, if symbolism is the name of the game, radical psychical deconstructing is necessary for Galatians 3.28 ('There is neither Jew nor Greek; there is neither slave nor free; there is no male and female, for you are all one') to become more than a desirable ideal.

When the Declaration on the Question of the Admission of Women to the Ministerial Priesthood appeared a decade later it simply added momentum to an already snowballing debate. Isolated voices combined into movements, and existing organizations joined in the argument. At the Council itself petitions had been put concerning the harmful effects of Aquinas' teaching on women, on the exclusion of women from the priesthood and on the canonical underpinning of this exclusion. St Joan's International Alliance,[6] which had been effective in its request to open council sessions to the female auditors, had passed a resolution in 1963 indicating that should the priesthood be opened to women, 'women would be willing and eager to respond'. The same organization in 1967 approached the World Congress of the Lay Apostolate to request a study on the role of women in the sacramental order and the church. Synods of various countries reiterated the plea that the question should be studied, yet although in 1975 the Vatican Study Commission on women in society and the church was set up, it was debarred from studying ordination. The Pontifical Biblical Commission and the International Theological Commission both embarked on studies in this field, and they passed their reports to the Sacred Congregation for the Doctrine of the Faith, which was responsible for the Declaration.

The wave of conciliar renewal sprang from societal movements from which also emerged the women's liberation movement of the 1970s. Renewal and liberation were keynotes for the second meeting of the Women's Ordination Conference which was held in Baltimore in 1978. There was animated debate as to whether conference resolutions should include the word 'ordination', because the concept was seen to need recognition, yet the word was finally retained lest the issue should be diffused. This debate was symbolically enacted in the final eucharistic celebrations – one in the main hall where a sympathetic man priest presided, and another in an adjoining hall where the women themselves shared presidency.

Present at the conference was a delegate from Roman Catholic Feminists, an organization which had been formed in England to unite and support women in the struggle against discrimination in the church. The members began a correspondence in the *Catholic Herald* on the ordination and language issues. In 1978 their clash with the Catholic Women's League at Westminster Cathedral during an 'equal rites' demonstration was reported in *The Times*,[7] and in 1979 they handed in a petition to Archbishop's House seeking an end to all discrimination on the grounds of sex.[8] They were invited to send a delegate to the National Pastoral Conference in Liverpool in 1980, where they declined to be in the 'role of women' group on the grounds that there was no role for women different from that of men, and joined the Justice and Peace sector. Interestingly their topic group passed a resolution that all structures of the church should reflect the participation of women in the preaching/ministerial function of the church by 37:7, while the admittance of women to the ministerial priesthood was rejected by 18:35 and the elimination of sexist language in the liturgy was also rejected by the even greater margin of 9:40.

This post-conciliar ferment had ecumenical dimensions. A pattern of strategic intervention can be discerned between the movement of women towards ordination in the Church of England and Roman Catholic pronouncements.[9] The year the Declaration was published the Archbishop of Canterbury had exchanged letters with Pope Paul VI on the issue: the following year the General Synod of the Church of England passed a resolution that there were 'no fundamental objections' to women as priests but declined to pass a motion to remove legal barriers. When the same motion came before the General Synod again in 1978, Cardinal Hume addressed the Synod to express his 'deep concern' at the passing of such a motion: his warning was seemingly heeded, because the motion was defeated. When eventually in 1988 draft legislation was generally approved, *pace* Roman Catholic persuasion, the papal encyclical *Mulieris Dignitatum* appeared, which reiterated the *in persona Christi* argument of the Declaration. It also followed an exchange of letters between the Pope and the Archbishop, on this occasion the correspondence initiated by John Paul II.

Final approval of ordination of women to the priesthood was given by the General Synod of the Church of England in November 1992. St Joan's International Alliance and the Catholic Women's Network put out a joint press statement to congratulate the synod. However, their joy was not shared in Vatican circles. Six years earlier, in 1987, the year in which Synod finally agreed to prepare draft legislation on the issue, the Vatican had broken with tradition in announcing the preparation of an encyclical. *Veritatis Splendor* was duly published in 1993, its aim seemingly to reassert that an objective morality exists, that it can be known and taught by the church, and that this is illustrated with statements on the nature of men and women. There is thus a shift from symbolic argument *per se* towards a claim to the authority to interpret and hence to construct perceptions of sexuality, which brings to mind the work of Foucault.[10] Analogously one recalls that *Humanae Vitae* centred on authority when the lock on the stable door appeared to have given way.[11] The canon to allow the ordination of women in the Church of England was promulgated on 22 February 1994, and the first women were ordained in Bristol on 12 March. Catholic Women's Ordination (CWO) was founded, inspired by the Church of England Movement for the Ordination of Women (MOW), and its protest at the loss to the church of women's gifts, symbolized by a purple veil, was pictured and described in *The Independent* later that month.

Then on 13 May the Pope released a letter to the bishops,[12] declaring it a 'definitive judgment' that the church has 'no authority whatsoever' to ordain women. He quotes from Paul VI's 1975 letter to the Archbishop:

[The Catholic Church] holds that it is not admissible to ordain women to the priesthood, for very fundamental reasons. These reasons include: the example recorded in the sacred Scriptures of Christ choosing his Apostles only from among men; the constant practice of the Church, which has imitated Christ in choosing only men; and her living teaching authority which has consistently held that the exclusion of women from the priesthood is in accordance with God's plan for his Church.

He then extends the argument to meet Catholic objections to the Declaration with a 'theological anthropology' which, he claims, is not culturally relative. By way of illustration he refers to the 'fact' that Mary did not receive the 'mission proper to the Apostles' nor the 'ministerial priesthood' to argue that neither slight nor discrimination against women can be construed from the official line. Seemingly we are faced with 'God's plan' and women's 'vocation', and this 'dignity' must be eagerly defended by 'the Church'. Although the letter did not explicitly mention the *in persona Christi* argument, it was clearly implied.

Following the ordination of women in the Church of England, a number of Church of England clergy have joined the Roman Catholic Church and asked to minister at the altar. The granting of such requests had led to raised eyebrows among Roman Catholic clergy who had married, and to whom such permissions have not been forthcoming. Cardinal Hume addressed this issue in a pastoral letter on 2 July 1995. This cross-movement of the disaffected has also led some people to link the word 'misogynist' with Roman Catholic practice. Perhaps in response to these criticisms, on 10 July 1995, John Paul II published a letter to women. However, many would argue that the apology contained within it falls short of the offence, because just as at the heart of *Mulieris Dignitatum* is a reiteration of the icon argument, so too a similar statement appears in the latest publication, although now the tone is more conciliatory:

If Christ – by his free and sovereign choice, clearly attested to by the Gospel and by the Church's constant Tradition – entrusted only to men the task of being an *'icon' of his countenance as 'shepherd' and 'bridegroom'* of the Church through the exercise of the *ministerial priesthood*, this in no way detracts from the role of women . . . [13]

Women continue to be theologized into a 'role' which is intrinsically other than that of men.

Officially, then, the affair has come full circle since Vatican II in the Roman Catholic Church as far as the priesthood issue is concerned. Hitherto taboo questions were brought to the surface; biblical, ecumenical, theological and symbolic arguments were raised against the ordination of women and all have been successfully refuted. Yet the debate has culminated in a definitive stand by the Vatican that women cannot be ordained. In the Church of England, on the other hand, since the 1960s the question has been raised, debated and subjected to democratic synodical procedures, and women have been received into the priesthood; undoubtedly the episcopate will eventually be opened as well. Clearly democratic processes stand over and against authoritarian pronouncements.

What then is ultimately being defended in the Roman Catholic Church? Is it a question of creeping infallibility or theological anthropology? Certainly infallibility is used as an ultimate tool to silence argument; its forging has been admirably described by Hasler in *How the Pope Became Infallible: Pius IX and the Politics of Persuasion*.[14] This tool is alluded to in order to prop up a theologized symbolic structure which failed to convince the Church of England through the icon argument, and which fails to convince a large number of Roman Catholic women and men who can see no reason why women should not be ordained to the priesthood.

The culmination of the christologico-theological argument is that a woman cannot image Christ as a priest acts *in persona Christi* at the moment of consecration. The identities woman-bride-church and man-bridegroom-Christ were taken up in a series of *L'Osservatore Romano* articles in the wake of the Declaration. Spiazzi writes:

> If the ministerial priesthood reflects the image of Christ, the head and bridegroom, the Christian woman is called to reflect in herself and reveal the identity of the bride-Church, the supreme type of which is a woman whose name is Mary . . . The principle of the 'eternal feminine' in Christianity did not clothe itself in myths, but became history in the Mary-Christ pair.[15]

Martelet in the same series argues that the ministerial priesthood is an efficacious sign of 'the Absent One', which points to 'the moment of complete communication between the Bridegroom and the Bride, which is, as is known, the Eucharist, the climax of the espousals of the whole

Church with her Lord'.[16] Inevitably gender differentiation leads to a high covert or overt concentration on sex. One recalls that an emphasis on biological motherhood was explicitly rejected by Jesus in favour of discipleship.[17]

The allegedly timeless argument that women and men are essentially different relates, as do all ideas, to a historical perspective, and can be linked to a social structure predating capitalism, where the roots of the institutional church are earthed. As the male became identified with God under patriarchy women came to symbolize the Other or what-differentiates-the-Subject.[18] This has been assimilated by Christian institutional structures. A decade prior to the Declaration, Mary Daly had become convinced that Christianity was irredeemably sexist and bad news for women. In *Beyond God the Father*[19] she argues that an existential leap across the abyss is necessary in order that women may encounter Be-ing and say 'I am'. She later traces the locus of women's bid for freedom outside patriarchal society – at the periphery – in a reforging of language. Yet is this creation of new vision and reality construction as advocated by Daly the only possible solution? Can unconscious forces and symbolic structures be deconstructed and reforged without so radical a break?

Perhaps Habermas' critical hermeneutics can throw some light on the subject when applied to New Testament texts.[20] Previously hermeneutics could not explain lies, censorship, the manipulation and oppression of thought and the force over people's minds exercised by ideological structures in the formation of false consciousness. Habermas went beyond Gadamer's fusion of horizons to analyse pseudo-communication in order to retrieve the meanings that are concealed in the language of texts.

Such a hermeneutical perspective has been taken up by Elisabeth Schüssler Fiorenza in her feminist reconstruction of Christian origins.[21] Her 'tentative and preliminary' reconstruction of the Jesus movement in Palestine as a prophetic movement centred on *basileia* distanced it from the cultic interpretation of associated symbols – for example the concept of holiness or the understanding of Jesus' death. She sees the *locus* of God's action away from cult towards all-inclusive community which would have attracted social marginals and thus particularly women. Jesus is remembered as Sophia who is put to death because of his challenge to imperialism. The pre-Gospel traditions are interpreted as addressing patriarchal structures, for example the controversy stories on patriarchal marriage, the a-familial ethos of the movement and the rejection of biological motherhood, and the exclusion of the power and status accorded to fathers: with 'father' is associated the gracious goodness usually associated with a mother and the rejection of patriarchal structures of domination. Schüssler Fiorenza then traces the patriarchalizing trajectory of the communities after Jesus' death. First Galatians 3.28 was qualified by Paul; then these qualifications were developed in the Deutero-Pauline codes and the Pastoral Epistles. However, while the majority of the communities succumbed to the patriarchalizing influences, the Gospels of Mark and John point to an alternative vision of community which emphasized love and service as the core of Jesus' ministry and the mark of discipleship. Although patriarchy was victorious, it is not rooted in the praxis of Jesus.

If one concedes that this reading of Christian origins is persuasive, then waves are definitely made. Institutional theologized symbolic structures must be deconstructed to recapture the spirit of the earliest communities. At the centre of the symbolic structure is 'he became man', which is at the root of the *in persona Christi* argument. Liturgical linguistic changes are merely cosmetic unless this phrase is addressed. I have argued elsewhere that the familiarity of Jesus' Abba prayer subverted the patriarchal structures in which he found himself.[22] The earliest baptismal formula of Galatians 3.28 understood this well.

Future projections are always suspect, because one cannot foresee future variables. The institutional church *may* have a change of heart, but when one considers the theological perspectives of the cardinals being created and the ascendency of Opus Dei in the Vatican, one must posit a totally unpredictable future variable if there is to be any reasonable hope for a change of heart. Yet Jesus and his community of disciples challenged imperial structures from the margins, and the depth of the challenge to the structures and unconscious associated symbols activated forces of resistance that culminated in Jesus' death. The early church understood this reversal, but the patriarchal structures of the wider society gradually impinged on the community for political reasons, culminating in the pre-Vatican II model. Perhaps we are now faced with two dialectically related possibilities. On the one hand we could look to the prototype of alternative Johannine and Gnostic communities to argue that whereas we know that Jesus' spirit remains with the community as he promised, he made no guarantee as to where the locus of this community was to be sited. On the other hand, we might look towards the challenge from Vatican II to the imperial structures of the church to suggest that in the light of a recognition of the false consciousness governing our acceptance of politicized christology and theology we can guard against their restoration and move towards the realization of Galatians 3.28 as an achievable ideal.

Notes

1. Walter M. Abbott (ed.), *The Documents of Vatican II*, London and New York 1966, 227–8.

2. 'Declaration on the Question of the Admission of Women to the Ministerial Priesthood' (*Inter Insigniores*), 1977.

3. Mary Daly, *The Church and the Second Sex*, Boston 1968.

4. Sister Vincent Emmanuel Hannon, *The Question of Women and the Priesthood*, London 1967.

5. *Pacem in Terris* 15.

6. In 1911 the Catholic Women's Suffrage Society was set up to secure the vote for women. In 1923 the name was changed to St Joan's Social and Political Alliance, and in 1931 to St Joan's International Alliance. The alliance has consultative status with the United Nations' Economic and Social Council, and is accredited to UNESCO.

7. *The Times*, 26 June 1978.

8. *The Guardian*, 1 May 1979.

9. Developed in Jacqueline Field-Bibb, *Women Towards Priesthood: Ministerial Politics and Feminist Praxis*, Cambridge 1991.

10. Michel Foucault, *The History of Sexuality 1, An Introduction*, Harmondsworth 1978.

11. See Hans Küng, *Infallible? An Enquiry*, London and New York 1994.

12. John Paul II, letter to bishops published in the *Tablet* (4 June 1994), 720–1.

13. 'Letter of Pope John Paul II to Women' (10 July 1995), para. 11.

14. August Bernard Hasler, *How the Pope Became Infallible: Pius IX and the Politics of Persuasion*, New York 1981.

15. Raimondo Spiazzi, 'The Advancement of Women According to the Church', *L'Osservatore Romano*, 10 February 1977, 6, 7.

16. Gustave Martelet, 'The Mystery of the Covenant and its Connections with the Nature of the Ministerial Priesthood', *L'Osservatore Romano*, 17 March 1977, 6, 7.

17. Developed in Elisabeth Schüssler Fiorenza, *In Memory of Her: A Feminist Theological Reconstruction of Christian Origins*, London and New York 1983, 176–7.

18. Developed in Field-Bibb, *Women Towards Priesthood* (n. 9), 261–89. See also the review by Mary Condren in *The Furrow* 43.2, 1992, 116–18.

19. Mary Daly, *Beyond God the Father: Towards a Philosophy of Women's Liberation*, Boston 1973 and London 1986.

20. See Josef Bleicher, *Contemporary Hermeneutics: Hermeneutics as Method, Philosophy and Critique*, London 1980.

21. Schüssler Fiorenza, *In Memory of Her* (n. 7). For an overview of reviews see Field-Bibb, *Women Towards Priesthood* (n. 9), 246–61.

22. Jacqueline Field-Bibb, '"By Any Other Name": The Issue of Inclusive Language', *Modern Churchman* 37.2, 1989, 5–9.

Concilium Round Table: The Impact of Feminist Theologies on Roman Catholic Theology

David Tracy

There can be little doubt that feminist thought has been the major challenge across the disciplines, including philosophy and theology. Indeed, the focus on gender (along with the equally important focus on race and class) has shifted the historical side of all disciplines (again including theology) from a more familiar concern with historical context to a more exact concern with 'social location' (gender, race, class) as necessary elements in any analysis of historical context. This methodological challenge, in turn, has linked gender studies to the emancipatory thrust of all critical theories and has linked feminist theologies and, in the USA context, moreover, African-American, womanist and mujerista theologies to the emergence, across the globe, of liberation movements and theologies.

This union of historical gender studies and liberationist commitments has changed the historical character of all theology. It is no longer possible to engage in serious historical work, from the scriptures to the contemporary period, and ignore gender issues: both to recover once forgotten, silenced, marginalized women's voices over the centuries and to develop important forms of a feminist hermeneutics of suspicion on the mainline tradition. It will probably take the work of several generations to complete this rethinking of the Christian tradition now occurring, with gender studies leading the analysis of new forms of hermeneutics of both retrieval and suspicion.

But rather than analysing further the crucial challenges which feminist and womanist theologies have made hermeneutically to all theology, I will now focus my attention on one specific example of the kind of challenge feminist thought has posed in my own discipline of fundamental theology.

Since fundamental theology characteristically analyses the relationships of 'faith' and 'reason' it becomes crucial, especially since modernity, to study the diverse meanings of modern rationality. The many contemporary forms of fundamental theology not influenced by feminist thought have ignored for too long how feminist thought (more than any other contemporary hermeneutic of suspicion on models of modern rationality) has challenged three central defects in the standard account of modern concepts of rationality.

It is now clear that modern notions of rationality (including the models employed in many contemporary forms of fundamental theology or, more generally, the apologetic side of all theology) have enforced three fatal separations: 'thought' was separated from feeling and experience; 'content' was separated from 'form'; modern 'theory' was separated from 'practice'.

In each of these cases, feminist thought has formulated the sharpest critiques and the most persuasive rethinkings. Feminist and womanist theologies have clarified how contextual all 'experience' is and how contingent and masculinist the separation of 'thought' from 'feeling' turns out to be. Hence the retrieval and rethinking of 'rhetoric' by so many feminist and womanist theologies.

Secondly, it is feminist thought that has most seriously challenged the dominance of narrow modern notions of rational argument and narrow modern notions of theory as the only proper form for 'reason' or 'rationality'. The recovery of the forms of song, lament, narrative, especially in womanist theologies, as well as the experimentation with new forms of theology itself, has broken the impasse, within fundamental theology, in separating form and content to analyse both 'faith' and 'reason'.

Third, feminist and womanist theologies, here joining all contemporary forms of political and liberation theology, have consistently insisted upon the need to link praxis and theory again – including relating the praxis of ethical-political action and concrete spiritual practices. Hence, the retrieval of 'spirituality' in so much feminist and womanist theology without the loss of ethical-political commitment and action: a genuinely mystical-political option.

In all these ways – and many more – feminist and womanist theologies have shifted all serious theological reflection. Once any theologian, female or male, understands the full impact and range of that challenge, there is no turning back to the former world of 'faith' and 'reason' – a world well-lost.

Marciano Vidal

My field of specialization is *theological ethics*, and more specifically the *fundamental* aspect of this. Taking stock of my theological-moral journey to the present, I can joyfully acknowledge that feminist theology and ethics have had a notable impact on my presentation of theological ethics. This is due basically to my reading of feminist works in the fields of theology and ethics, but also to the influence that women have had on me, above all the religious I have counted among my students at the university and on various courses I have taught in a large number of countries.

The impact of feminism on my conception of theological ethics can be grouped under three headings:

1. *'Sexual difference' or, rather, 'gender' in moral anthropology*. For years I have been trying to change the casuistic treatise 'On Human Acts' to 'Moral Anthropology'. Into this anthropological basis of morality I introduced, as one of its dimensions, what I called the principle of 'sexual difference', and what I now call a 'sex-gender schema'. In the first (1974) edition of *Moral Fundamental personalista*, I spoke of sexual difference as one of the 'coordinates of a person's being and purpose' (pp. 185–91). I proposed the active presence of women both in the moral 'life' (*ethica utens*) and in moral 'theory' (*ethica docens*). On this point I wrote: 'Many moral problems would have had a different expression and a different solution if they had also been considered from the feminine angle' (p. 190). In the last (6th, 1990) edition, I continue to uphold the same position, but better documented from recent reading (pp. 347–54).

2. *Women as the 'content' of moral theology in history and the present*. From the above statement, I proceeded to study how women have been treated in the history of moral theology. In 1981 I published a study of 'Women and Ethics' ('Mujer y ética', *Moralia* 3, 29–55). In this I evidenced the 'negative', 'pre-scientific' and 'ideological' treatment of women from the time of the Fathers to recent years; my study was inspired by the work of the woman theologian K. E. Børresen. I re-worked this study for volume II, part 2 of *Moral de Actitudes*, titled 'The Morality of Love and Sexuality' (1991). With new data (here I acknowledge a debt to Uta Ranke-Heinemann) and new approaches (learned at least in part from my *Concilium* colleagues Elisabeth Schüssler-Fiorenza and Lisa Sowle Cahill), I have tried to construct a critical assessment of the past and to make a constructive proposal for the future (pp. 225–49).

3. *Properly feminist ethics*. The Spanish Association of Theologians held its first Congress on the subject of 'Ethics and Women' in Madrid in June 1993. I was invited to give a paper, which involved me in studying the

most recently-produced works on feminist ethics. These are abundant, treating the subject either from the perspective of 'feminism of equality' or from that of 'feminism of difference'. I took stock of C. Gilligan's proposal of a feminine ethics of 'care' as opposed to the masculine ethics of 'justice'; it seemed to me that the best solution was a fusion of the two. I also dialogued with other protagonists of 'difference' (L. Irigaray) and, more specifically, with those of 'maternal thinking' (S. Ruddick). Without denying the contributions of this approach from difference, the ethical perspective that stems from the feminism of equality (S. Benhabib) seems to me to be richer. I have also taken account of other contributions, both from Spain (C. Amorós, V. Camps, A. Valcárcel, M. Navarro) and from other countries (B. H. Andolsen, M. Hunt, V. Adriana, M. Dimais, M. Nussbaum, M. Farley). I set out the results of my inquiry into properly feminist ethics in two articles published in the review *Razón y Fe* 228 (1993), 147–66, and 229 (1994), 78–92. In analysing feminist ethics, I have taken theological ethics as a reference. I see the latter as in need of not only a thorough 'feminization', but also a strong 'feminist critique'. I do not exclude the possibility of further articles on these subjects.

Translated by Paul Burns

Norbert Mette

With its post-Idealist paradigm, which sees the present practical context (the historical and social context) as constitutive for the formation of theories, feminist theology shows a high degree of affinity with the practical section of theology, which understands itself as critical reflection on church or community praxis in society. So it is not surprising that feminist theology – like liberation theology – has produced important stimuli for the further clarification of the approach and status of this theological discipline. Special mention should be made of its contribution in making more precise an appropriate theological understanding of practice that sees even church and community action as no longer detached from the tensions and conflicts of the society in which it is set, confronting it explicitly with the challenges posed by that society.

Here the traditional ecclesiocentric reduction of church or pastoral activity, and even more its attachment to persons officially appointed (and ordained) for it, who are regarded as its normative subjects, is broken through – in favour of understanding the activity as the 'ministry of reconciliation' (II Cor. 5.18), offered together and in solidarity in a world which is divided, not least in terms of gender.

However, this new definition of the concept of praxis in practical theology, within the framework of a more comprehensive individual and collective praxis of liberation, does not mean that the question of the problem of the status of women in the churches and communities is being elegantly disguised. On the contrary, precisely in the context of the struggle for women's emancipation which is being carried on all over the world, the more or less blatant outdatedness of church praxis stands out all the more vividly, and with it the church's 'theory' (ideology) in this respect. Ultimately this means that the church is not doing justice to its mission to be 'a sign and instrument of communion with God and of unity among all humankind' (*Lumen Gentium* 1). That this calls for a fundamental change in church praxis, in the sense of biblical *koinonia*, is an insight which meanwhile has also come to be shared widely within practical theology and which that theology is concerned to implement.

Here the male representatives of this discipline, who at present are dominant in it, as in other branches of theology (though there is a substantial proportion of women in the rising generation of practical theologians), have taken up many of the demands of feminist theologians. In an awareness that even the presence of a far larger number of women in positions of responsibility in the church does not necessarily change church praxis, they have engaged in individual initiatives in research into male attitudes and done practical work in this area. For sometimes feminist approaches have also become established, particularly in religious education. Here a promising sphere of research and practice is opening up: this involves not only the practical question of an appropriate socialization and upbringing for boys and girls, young men and women, but also the promotion of basic research which goes beyond theology into the genesis and development of the female – as opposed to the male – religious sense.

Julia Ching

Some people work in the mainstream of society, and others on the so-called periphery. Were I a China scholar working in China a hundred years ago, I might have been in the mainstream, except that it would not have been possible for a woman to be doing so. Were I a China scholar in today's China, I would expect not to be in the mainstream, because the country is too preoccupied with making money, and puts humanities at the bottom of its academic totem pole. Fortunately, I am a China scholar working in the West, and that means, on the periphery of the academic scene.

I happen also to be a scholar of religion, including comparative religion. And here, I still remain on the periphery, because most people, even in the West, place more value on Wall Street than on religion and culture, especially what people consider to be the exotic kind of studies. But my involvement in *Religionswissenschaft* has persuaded me that the principal religions of the world are all patriarchally based.

The work done in feminist theology has alerted people like myself to another way of looking at things than the mainstream way, even of seeking to change what is the mainstream. I myself am now orientating my research on more relevant aspects, regarding questions of gender, of population, of reproductive health, and of the environment. And I am looking at the past, including the past legacies of the world's great religions, much more critically in these terms.

I am also realizing that the crimes and mistakes committed by patriarchy in the past and present were and are often committed not just by the men, but also sometimes by their willing partners, the women. Whether out of emotions of fear or desire for power, women, as well as men, have sought to dominate other women and men.

If I may express one small hope, it is that women and men will work together to change the patriarchy that continues to dominate the life of the Church and of theology.

William R. Burrows

In September 1972, I arrived in Papua New Guinea with a new licentiate in theology from the Gregorian University. I had been assigned to teach at the regional Catholic seminary near Port Moresby by my superiors in the Society of the Divine Word. I knew I had a great deal to learn about Melanesian culture. What I did not know was that the religious women of two congregations, the Sisters of Mercy and the Missionary Servants of the Holy Spirit, were going to teach me equally much about how the world changes when you take women's insights seriously. What I learned from their perspectives and about the difficulty of men and women attaining a common horizon on ecclesial issues and responses to the gospel has only deepened since 1972. My sense that men and women in the church need much more dialogue has not changed.

In 1972 we were newly appropriating the theology of Vatican Council II. In that context, I gave a number of theological conferences on ministry, retreats and recollections; often to groups of men alone, of women alone, and, more rarely, of men and women together. I began reading work by theologians such as Valerie Saiving, Mary Daly and Rosemary Ruether in response to what the women missionaries were bringing up. At one level I found feminist theology helpful, but at another I realized that what I was taking from their writing was different from what the women were finding there.

At the first level, it was possible to analyse the difference as follows: women were very concrete about reshaping the church to meet human needs and were impatient with abstractions; men were defensive and wanted to consider implications of various ideas and to consider all the ramifications of adopting a train of ideas. At the second level, it was clear that each group was wary about the other's fundamental approach. It was even clearer that, because the power structure was so overwhelmingly male, women were not being dealt with fairly.

During doctoral studies at the University of Chicago, I would become more sophisticated about hermeneutics and communications horizons and what happens when they are systematically distorted. Having left religious life and married a skilled psychotherapist, I also began to see how different were women's approaches to problems. The book that finally gave me a key to what was going on in the church and its theological meaning, though, was Elisabeth Schüssler Fiorenza's *In Memory of Her*. It led me to interpret the institutional church's actions to censor what women were saying on ordination policies, ethics and liturgy as a repetition in a new setting of the dramatic suppression of women's voices in the first century.

Feminist thought led me to judge that we live in a dysfunctional church that cannot properly manifest Christ as God's Sophia, the world's light, nor minister to the world's problems. By that I mean that an ideological position at the church's hierarchical pinnacle suppresses honest discussion of serious issues. In the first century that suppression took place because Mediterranean society as a whole supported the suppression. As we enter the twenty-first century, the cultural situation will not permit this suppression again.

As part of the publishing world, I watch with alarm the enfeeblement of institutional Catholicism and the estrangement of so many from it, largely caused by failing to pay attention to women's issues. The dysfunctionality of the church means that men and women cannot honestly debate issues publicly, so they can profit from each other's insights and correct each other's distortions. Catholic publishers are, in my opinion, witnessing the disintegration of the classical *ager publicus* and church that wanted to read a Rahner, a Guardini, or a Congar who painted attractive pictures of discipleship options. Instead of being an aesthetic deepening and refining commitment in images friendly to both men's and women's hopes for the future, theology today is too often a conceptual enterprise bickering about backward ecclesiastical sexual politics.

Feminist theology, I believe, correctly identified sexism as a core block to honest discourse about our situation. Along with racism and social class inequities, sexism must be confronted. If it is not, very little else that troubles us will be. For completeness, though, no one group of women's voices can predominate. A wide variety of women's voices from many cultures must be heard, just as there needs to be intelligent male conversation with those voices. I still believe the lesson taught me by a handful of Melanesian, Australian and German women in the mid-1970s in Papua New Guinea: hearing the voice of women is one of the chief ways our world and church will begin to discuss the full range of things necessary to bring health to humankind.

III · Different Theoretical Sites of Struggle

South Asian Feminist Theory and its Significance for Feminist Theology

Gabriele Dietrich

I Some relationships in need of clarification

The present article tries to address itself to some significant concepts and issues of South Asian feminist theory and to explore their relevance for feminist theologizing. In this, no attempt can be made to be comprehensive or representative for the South Asian countries. Being located in South India, my main experience relates to India, especially the South, and up to a point Sri Lanka. Pakistan and Bangladesh are only marginally dealt with, though certainly the major debates overlap the boundaries of countries.

To come to grips with the relationship of secular feminist theory and feminist theology, some peculiarities of the region need to be taken into account.

First of all, feminist theology is socially visible only in the south of India as well as Sri Lanka, where larger Christian minorities form part of the population. Even then, feminist theology has not been perceived by the women's movement as a discipline putting forward serious methodological issues. Nor has secular feminist theory been perceived much in feminist theology. The reasons for this are not far to seek. All the South Asian countries have religious majority cultures which gravitate in different degrees towards establishing the majority culture as a state religion. Even India, though technically still a secular state, has gone far along the way of becoming a 'Hindu nation'.

Secondly, 'women's studies' has become established as an academic discipline, in the wake of the two decades after International Women's Year. However, feminist theory is not necessarily predominant in such academic departments, as they tend to shun the in-depth analysis of patriarchy and focus much more on 'gender studies' and empirical research about women. In India, some of the theological colleges like TTS, Gurukul and recently UTC have departments of women's studies, but women here often find it difficult to uphold a feminist perspective within the extremely male dominated faculties and student bodies. The difference and connection between women's studies and feminist theology is often unclear. Independent institutions like the Centre for Society and Religion, Colombo, have made an impact on the Catholic Church up to a point by putting forward feminist theology, and on the Catholic side in India groups like WINA (catering to laywomen) and WORTH (formed by religious sisters) have generated discussions and materials. WORTH in particular has done serious work in discussing Western theological positions and analysing Hindu mythological materials.

Thirdly, despite the fact that women's studies often lack feminist teeth, and feminist theology either draws on Western imports or tends to remain entirely experiential or narrative, there is a significant ferment created by a body of theoretical debate which is located and rooted mainly in the activist scene of the women's movement. These debates surface, for instance, in the bi-annual meetings of the Indian Association of Women's Studies (IAWS), which gives room for activists as a matter of principle and in activist conferences and workshops, some of which are international within the region.

Fourthly, what this body of debate means for feminist theology needs to be examined. This is not easy, as feminist theology in South Asia has not clarified itself much in its relationship to liberation theology in general or dalit theology in particular, despite having a commitment to the poor and oppressed. The present article only outlines some of the significant issues and concepts raised, without being able to outline in any detail the theological methodology which would be adequate to respond to these issues and conceptualizations.

II Some key issues and related concepts

1. The concept of feminism itself

There is controversy about the concept in the first place. Often it has been suggested by liberal as well as Marxist critics that feminism is in itself a 'Western' concept which cannot be directly applied in Asia.[1] This has partly to do with the fact that feminism emerged in some of our countries as a reaction to certain aspects of party politics, especially of the Left. For this reason, for the generation of feminists who became active in the late 1960s and early 1970s it was connected with the vision of a new economic order, human relations with nature, a classless society. This means there has been a strong socialist feminist mainstream in South Asia. In more recent years, the question of peasants, dalits and women and ecology got connected. For this reason, not only did the question of patriarchy, caste and class get addressed in an integrated way, but the overall question of transformation of society was ever-present. Therefore, the question constantly needs to be addressed whether the basic demands relate only to what one would put under the label of equity feminism or whether a fundamentally different type of development is envisaged. In other words, are we addressing questions of equal rights only or are we envisaging a fundamentally different perspective on each and every issue and aspect of society? A more liberal type of equity feminism has in some ways been integrated by the state in the wake of the UN Decade of Women. This approach can also be found in many NGOs which work on gender awareness and gender justice and often co-operate closely with the state. On the other hand, the need for much more fundamental transformation is strongly felt by unions in the informal sector, dalits, adivasis, peasants and some of the ecological movements. Obviously, all of this is theologically relevant. This debate helps us to see more critically what is happening with respect to women in the churches.

The South Asian churches have up to a point addressed themselves to questions of women's ordination and gender-just language; they also unavoidably have to address the problem of mass poverty in their midst, and much of feminist theology has a definite option for the poor. However, the barriers between dalit theology and feminist theology have not been broken down. As large parts of the dalit movements have a perception that feminism is a middle-class, upper-caste urban phenomenon, dalit theologians also insist on the primacy of caste discrimination, and do not work out the connection between caste and patriarchy very clearly. In contrast to this, over the past five years the women's movement has begun very seriously to address caste and communal issues, and autonomous organizations of dalit women are coming forward strongly. This is a learning process which has not yet been reflected in the perceptions of church and theology.

2. Ecology and control over resources. Production of life

In South Asia, there is an intensive thinking process going on over the ecological question. This has to do with resistance against big dams (e.g. Sarvar Sarovar on the Narmada, Tehri dam in Garhwal, Mahaveli in Sri Lanka) as well as with movements to save the forest and protect the rights of forest dwellers, and with the survival struggle for water. In 1990 the National Forum of Fishworkers (NFF) in India organized the coastal march Protect Waters, Protect Life all along the eastern and western coast of India. Massive agitations against foreign licensing have been going on, and prawn cultivation is a main target of protest.

As Bina Agarwal has been pointing out,[2] the Indian experience has thrown up a different kind of perspective, which she terms feminist environmentalism as opposed to a more Western-inspired formulation of eco-feminism, which is closer to concepts of 'deep ecology'. While eco-feminism in the West has tended to focus on the close nexus between 'women' as a general category, the Indian debate has brought forward much more in depth the class reality of poor peasant women who are marginalized by the hegemonic development process. In brief, the following ingredients can be identified: 'An alternative approach, suggested by feminist environmentalism, needs to be *transformational* rather than welfarist – where development, redistribution and ecology link in mutually regenerative ways. This would necessitate complex and inter-related changes such as in the *composition* of what is produced, the *technologies* used to produce it, the *processes* by which decisions on products and technologies are arrived at, the *knowledge-systems* on which such choices are based, and the class and gender distribution of products and tasks.'[3] This means that a transformational ecofeminism or feminist environmentalism need to go in detail into alternative economics. It raises the question of what is produced, how and for whom, how is it processed and marketed and the organizational aspects required for alternative patterns of production, as well as the movements which will have to fight for forces of the state, which pushes the hegemonic ecologically destructive development model.

This kind of approach is fairly close to the writings of Maria Mies and Vandana Shiva, who have made a wide impact in the international debate, basing themselves on the Indian experience.[4] However, their conceptual-ization is considerably more sweeping in connecting women's subsistence production with a spirituality of reconciliation with Mother Earth and a scathing criticism of Western science and technology as patriarchal and colonial. We have therefore been accused of ecological myth-making.[5] Some of this criticism raises the question how caste/class aspects are worked out in their approach, and how much the scathing critique of Western individualism is warranted in the face of the fact that the patriarchal culture in the communities involved in struggles to save the forest dominates the movement as well, and suffocates its feminist aspiration. Again, the need to raise organizational questions is imperative.

This has been done in exemplary ways by Chhaya Datar[6] in her position paper for the RC 32 Session 16 and 17 at the International Sociology Congress in Bielefeldt in July 1994. Chhaya very clearly distinguishes between two fundamentally different strategies among feminists. One integrates women into the 'mainstream' characterized by growth orientation, consumerism, hi-tech, emphasis on market, centralization of market forces, emphasis on women's participation in public life. The other redefines development, which is focussed upon women's activity in survival and subsistence economy, sharing of natural resources, production for basic needs as opposed to wants, security of food and shelter, decentralized production and marketing process with democratic participation. This envisages alternative technology characteristic of an agriculture focussed on a post-heavy industry production process and decentralized rural industries based on developed artisanal skills and local resources.

A crucial conceptualization in which some of these attempts are summed up is that of the 'production of life' rather than production for profit. In the South Asian workshop on Women and Development in January 1989, in which twenty-three prominent women activists from the countries of the region came together, this was formulated as follows:

'Production of Life' includes not only the bearing and rearing of children but also the basic sustenance of life in subsistence production, household labour, informal sector, basic ecological activities which preserve forest cover, water systems, energy and the ozone layer. We prefer this concept to the traditional Marxist conceptualization which sees these basic life-processes as 're-production', while 'production' is seen as extended production for the market and for accumulation of capital. We affirm the production of life as the basis of all other economic processes. It is obvious that a struggle which puts production of life at the centre is by definition anti-capitalist, anti-imperialist and critical of mechanistic solutions which modern, Western science and technology may try to offer as a panacea for the ecological breakdown of the planet. It is also profoundly different from the development concepts which have been followed by actually existing socialism. This relates us to the whole feminist ecological debate which tries to redefine 'productivity', 'work and leisure', Gross Natural Product v. Gross National Product, parameters of work input and participation, relationship between the unorganized and organized sectors, need-based v. want-based production, and so on.[7]

This also presupposes a deep connection between nature and women's bodies, women and health and government policies on sensitive issues like forest, water, health and population.[8]

What does all this imply for feminist theology? It will require not only integration of caste/class perspective with patriarchy, but also a creation theology which relates itself to the whole process of human labour. Besides, while Asian theologies have been more cosmological and focussed on the inter-connectedness of all forms of life, as well as spirituality, the feminist ecological experience compels us to look into the concrete circumstances in which the natural balance is disturbed, access to water, soil and means of survival undermined etc. Thus, ecological theological reflection needs to also include the critique of mammon, the consumerist middle-class ethos of the churches, the sharing miracles as connected to food security, water as a common property resource, the Earth as God-given and therefore not private property, the critique of administrative hierarchies, the integrity of the good creation as opposed to bio-technology, sex determination and female foeticide, the symbolisms of the seed and the tree of life as opposed to the activities of multi-national seed companies and deforestation.

3. The question of religion, communalism, fundamentalism

Feminist theology in South Asia finds itself in a situation where Christianity itself is a small minority religion *vis-à-vis* a state which either promotes a state religion or, as in India, gravitates towards increasing assertion of the majority culture. Not only that, women of the region are divided by religious family laws! Because of the overwhelming presence of patriarchal religion in women's lives, there has been a tendency in all the South Asian countries to view religion as a destructive and oppressive force.

As I have worked out much more extensively elsewhere,[9] an incisive debate on the possible liberating and sustaining aspects of religion first arose in the national conference of the autonomous women's movements held in Bombay in 1986. This opened up the possibility of taking cognizance of feminist Christian theology. However, such interaction did not take place, partly because of the latent majority communalist implications of the secular women's movement itself. This point was forcefully driven home by Flavia Agnes, a feminist lawyer, at the conference of the National Association of Women's Studies in Yadavpur in 1991, where she characterized the underlying majority communalist assumptions in the secular women's movement and, for the first time in the history of the IAWS, made public reference to Christian liberation theology/feminist theology as a tool of cultural liberation in a plenary session of the association.

The ensuing debate was heavy and emotion-charged, as it confronted all the participants in great depth with their religious identity and community. However, the focus did not shift to the methodology of dealing with religious texts or symbols, e.g. the question of women reappropriating their religious heritage in a radical perspective. The reasons for this are not far to seek. From the late 1980s onwards, with the increasing spread of communalism and fundamentalism in India, much to the consternation of the women's movement, women were seen to join more actively the ranks of communal and fundamentalist organizations, even though these were blatantly patriarchal. Not only that, women were also seen not only tolerating but themselves actively inflicting violence on other women belonging to the minority community. It became necessary to examine why for women the communal identification, though patriarchal, seemed to harbour more promise than the solidarity of the women's movement. The reasons are largely twofold. In general, the communal organization enables women to participate in public life with the support of the menfolk and elderly women of their community. As far as the minority community is concerned, especially among themselves, the fundamentalist organization becomes a vehicle of political assertion which safeguards the very right to survive and to fight for political sovereignty. For the sake of this right, even restrictive dress codes and norms of behaviour become acceptable,[10] as has been seen among the militant movement for the independence of Kashmir. For the majority community, the communal organization becomes a vehicle of asserting relative independence even in dress and life style, a place where identity can be found and asserted and an ideological vehicle to canalize aggression and national pride.

Paola Bacchetta has made this semi-Fascist brand of women's liberation strikingly visible in her research on women in the RSS.[11]

Such observations raise some serious questions about the ways feminist theology in India goes about inculturation. The tendency is to respond to the influence of Western feminist discourse on Goddess religion and to have recourse to female prototypes in the Hindu pantheon. For example, Catholic sisters having to cope with a thoroughly patriarchal environment and theological discourse tend to speak in terms of Shakti, Saraswathi, Mariamma etc. as feminine expressions of the divine and to analyse mythologies according to how they empower or subordinate women.[12] This does not call into question the connotation of such symbols in the upsurge of Hindu majority communalism. Empowerment within a potentially Fascist framework may be very injurious to the women's cause. We are also compelled to examine the problem that solidarity with Muslim women is by definition excluded in such symbolism. How can such political appropriation and distortion be dealt with?

There is no one clear answer to this question, since *any* religious symbolism can be distorted by oppressive political appropriation, as the history of Christianity itself amply shows. However, a partial answer lies in the awareness of the social origin and functioning of such symbols historically and in the present day with respect to the life-worlds of the different religious communities, channels of communication, formation of ideology and relationship to the larger systems of society which make an impact on these life-worlds.

This leads us back to the perception of the social structures and the life-worlds in which religious expressions are culturally embedded. It is interesting to note that on the whole, most feminist organizations in India have been extremely reluctant and restrained to draw on goddess symbolism because of the above-mentioned political constellation.

At the same time, there has been sustained interest in the exploration of women bhakti saints. The Indian magazine *Manushi* celebrated its ten years of existence with a special issue on women bhaktars. This interest has been more systematically worked out in a deeply significant study by Parita Mukta on Mirabai, the early sixteenth-century saint of Rajasthan who was devoted to Lord Krishna and who, in the strength of this love, not only rejected the authority of her husband, the ruler of Chittoor, but the whole martial, casteist, feudal ethos of the Rajputs, which was deeply inimical to women and people of lower castes. Mirabai, opting out of the privileged life at the court of Chittoor, had to cope with attempts to murder her and was facing severe social ostracism. Taking to a Chamar (leather worker) guru, Rohidas, the oral tradition of her songs became the medium of value assertion for artisanal castes, peasants and dalits, especially in Saurashtra, where Mira had migrated. She becomes part of 'a group of the under-privileged who are tied to each other by a distinct set of values that affirm a simple life uncorrupted by wealth and privilege. It is a group which deems that the good, the just, cannot flow from those exercising power and force. The members of this group are tied to each other by a system of morality and a system of values which uphold a community of like minds and hearts, held together by a sharing of common purpose. In the Mira bhakti, the tension and the power of these values is provided by the fact that Mira had to fight hard to retain her affiliation to a life of simplicity."[13] This study of Parita Mukta is theologically significant in a number of ways. She does not analyse the written texts of Mira bhakti but traces Mira through the medium of the orally transmitted culture of the communities, to whom the bhajan sessions are an affirmation of an identity and a way of life. Tracing the tradition in specific caste groups, she identifies the aspects of production, legitimation and motivation. Thus, she works out an ethos of frugality in the artisanal and peasant classes which blatantly challenges the legitimacy of the hegemonic patriarchal family and caste values of the Rajputs and in this transmits an ongoing motivation for protest and assertion, for an alternative social identity up to the present day.

This is not only significant as a methodology of research which is directly relevant for theologizing, but also forcefully affirms an ethos which is diametrically opposed not only to the traditions of feudalism but also to the values of consumerism, competition, reification and cultural nivellation which spread like wildfire in the wake of the new economic policies. We are very close here to some of the essential values of the Jesus community. Parita Mukta also shows concisely how the same tradition of Mira bhajans was blunted and deprived of its anti-patriarchal and anti-family sting by Gandhiji during the freedom struggle and how finally Mira today is being commercialized through movies and comic strips by the middle classes. However, this in no way takes away the forcefulness of the social protest of the poor bhajniks, but on the contrary accentuates it. Far beyond deconstruction or reconstruction of mere texts, and far beyond a merely biographical narrative approach to the person of Mira, we find a reconstruction of the ethos and the life world of the community of bhajniks to whom the very organization of the bhajan sessions becomes a medium which constitutes identity and social affirmation.

4 The question of violence: domestic, communal, economic and direct warfare

In South Asia, we have been forced to face the question of violence in an integrated way which does not allow us to draw neat boundaries between domestic violence, public rowdyism, communal and caste violence and ethnic warfare. This means that violence against women and other forms of violence which involve whole communities must be analysed in all their interlinkages.

On the one hand this has been made visible in the biographies of some of our most outstanding feminists; on the other, it has also gone into the conceptualizations of different movements. Within the brief space available, only a glimpse can be had of the depths of the overall problematic.

During the 1970s, when the rape question catapulted the Indian women's movement into action, the scourge of domestic violence was first made visible in very explicit ways by Flavia Agnes, who was then with Forum Against Oppression of Women.[14] She not only exposed her own biography as a battered wife to the public but contributed a great deal through writing and speeches towards tackling violence against women. She later became a lawyer to assist women to fight violence on their own.

During the 1990s, she has moved into work against communal violence and significantly contributed to organizational work during the Bombay riots after the destruction of the Babri Masjid in Ayodhya in December 1992. The organizations which supported her, i.e. the Forum as well as the Lawyers Collective and later Majlis, a legal cultural organization, have gone deep into the overall connections between the different forms of violence. Discussions on the interconnections between the different forms of violence have also taken place over the years in the magazine *Manushi*.[15]

These observations link us back with the painful events in Sri Lanka over the past twenty years, where military and ethnic violence has taken a heavy toll of the social fabric. One of the most outstanding contributions to feminist theory and praxis has come from Rajani Rajasingham, a doctor and human rights activist of extraordinary courage and integrity. She devoted her energies to the social reconstruction of the Tamil community in Jaffna, not least by co-founding the University Teachers for Human Rights (UTHR) and later the Poorani Women's Centre. The book *The Broken Palmyra*, which she co-authored with Rajan Hoole, K. Sridharan and Daya Somasundaram, gives a meticulous documentation of the violence not only of the Sri Lankan Army and the IPKF but also of all the Tamil groups. It was this insistence not to apply double standards which made her a target of the LTTE and cost her her life.[16] In her meticulous accounts of violence Rajani also analysed the role of women within the militant groups, their relative empowerment in the armed struggle, their compulsion to uncover human rights violations, the chauvinistic tendency to push women into the role of 'brave and valiant mothers', and the tendency of Tamil society to disown such women all the same. Most significantly, despite the extensive documentation of atrocities, women do not appear as victims in this account, but as those who have questioned, braved the guns and protected the community. In this attempt to assert life, ethnic boundaries are transcended and state power stands exposed side by side with the Indian army and the Fascist tendencies within the LTTE and other groups.

We are facing a situation here where traditional Marxist positions which locate patriarchy mainly in the relations of production and a radical feminist approach which would focus more on the autonomy of patriarchal violence are transcended. On the one hand, the role of the state in legitimizing and perpetuating violence becomes overwhelmingly clear, while at the same time, the violent structure of the life world, the day-to-day social structures of survival, of culture, of language, of communications, become painfully visible. Gail Omvedt has traced such connections in the debates emerging out of dalit movements and peasant movements in

Maharashtra.[17] Vandana Shiva has brought out the connection between the State, technocratic development policies and communalization of politics in her book on the Punjab situation.[18]

The recent upsurge of mass movements against alcoholism has made the linkage between domestic violence, a construction of the lifeworld and policies of the state visible in a different way.

Why and how are these connections theologically relevant? Christian feminists in the region are facing the challenge to address themselves fully to the politics of transformation which connects the violence of the hegemonic development concept, ethnic, caste and communal violence eroding the social fabric and militarizing political life with the 'ordinary' day-to-day violence against women in their daily life-world. This requires a shift of emphasis from the attempt to achieve equal rights, empower women, especially poor women, etc., towards an in-depth analysis of the root causes of deepening poverty and a theory of human needs which redeems the fall of the good creation in the light of table-fellowship for all. This cannot be an abstract postulate, but needs to be a very conscious process of the reorganization of society itself, in which feminist theologizing needs to locate itself and take part.

III The organizational question

In each and every part of this article, confronting the organizational question has become imperative. It will therefore be helpful to look at the organizational question in some more detail and to spell out some of the more important aspects. In an earlier article entitled 'The World As The Body of God', I tried to theologize directly on women's experiences in the slum-dwellers' and fish-workers' movements.[19] While I got the feedback that these theological reflections were inspiring and directly accessible because of their immediate and virtually poetic quality, it was also pointed out to me that it was not self-evident why reflection on people's movements should be of crucial theological importance. In the following some attempt is made to clarify the connections.

1. Life world – systems – people's movements[20]

In traditional societies, the horizon of interaction was dominated by the coherence of life worlds which were mediated by local languages and cultures, and in which legitimacy was reinforced by religious beliefs and rituals. While the state would superimpose systems of administration and commerce, this would leave the social structures largely untouched. Such non-interference can be observed even in the colonial policies of the British

Raj, where the day-to-day culture of survival, the family, the caste system and the religious life remained largely untouched. However, with the onslaught of modern science and technology and electronic communications, these systems of the state, the multinational corporations, international media, the international monetary system have permeated daily life and rapidly dissolved the social structures of the life world. While this has sometimes led to a certain weakening of traditional patriarchal structures, it has invited and reinforced more efficient modernized forms of colonial and neo-colonial patriarchy and has also dissolved structures of traditional solidarity which safeguarded survival and cultural cohesiveness, despite the costs of patriarchal, caste-, class- and age-based inequalities.

While historically people's movements have taken the shape of religious reform embodied in peasant's movements, and later of artisanal guilds and trade unions, the present-day situation catalyses movements into new shapes and into more crucial positions. They depend on the life world for recruiting membership and also empower the life world to renew itself and to resist the onslaught of totalitarian systems and social disintegration. Without the interaction of progressive social movements, the life world will either easily disintegrate – as has happened in many Western countries – or it will fossilize into rigid patriarchal and chauvinistic forms which project religions, ethnic or caste-based community identity at the cost of women, children and all democratically-minded sections. Without drawing on the traditional solidarities of the life world, movements will become culturally uprooted, ideologically abstract and out of touch with the humanistic contents of day-to-day survival. This also implies that the struggle for an alternative economy which is implied in the struggle for the hegemony of production of life over production for profit will have to be located in the interaction between life world and social movements.

2. Family–caste–community

In the present situation of economic and political crisis, the organizational forms of the life world face an identity crisis and a crisis of legitimation. Families are torn apart under the impact of the hegemonic development concept; caste identities, evened out by industrialism and city life, get reaffirmed in violent clashes in villages, in the unavoidable struggles about reservation and even in the organizational processes of the dalit movements. Religious community, under the pressures of the scarcity of resources and the onslaught of the media, takes on more and more communal connotations. Movements are cast in-between.

The women's movement, with its bitter experience of patriarchy and scathing critique of the family, finds itself at times in the same boat as the forces of modernity which dismantle the family. At the same time, women's subsistence survival base is destroyed by these same forces and women end up as sex objects and prostitutes.

The dalit movements, avowedly out to dismantle the caste system, find themselves reinforcing caste and getting split among each other along caste lines; finally they can end up being co-opted by communal forces. Communalization of politics reinforces an aggressive patriarchal structure, but at the same time offers free spaces for women to find a semblance of emancipation with the blessing of the religious community and a protected kind of identity.

Opening the debate on each of these issues and at the same time allowing the life world to reorganize itself creatively, without traditionalist pressures but also free from atomizing individualism, is a vital task for the survival for our humanness.

3. The role of the state

In the process outlined above, the role of the state has to be put in question afresh. In the post-independence period of South Asia, for a while there was a hope that the state might be able to safeguard and strengthen democratic spaces. This hope has undergone severe strains under conditions of military regimes, emergency and civil war. All of this has affected the life worlds of daily survival and women's spaces in society very adversely. After the UN decade on women, even now the South Asian states have not signed the Convention on Elimination of All Forms of Discrimination against Women (CEDAW). At the same time, the state co-opts people's movements and women's movements to implement its own development programmes. Feminists are using such spaces, while at the same time the resource situation deteriorates and the daily survival struggles of women are getting harsher. The state is abdicating more and more of its responsibility for infrastructure and social welfare, and at the same time taking an active part in the communalization of politics.

Nobody can do theology in a neutral space any more. We are in the middle of the survival struggle, the co-optation, the communalization of politics. Concern for priority, survival rights, freedom of religion, much of this may appear as a lost cause before long unless our interventions are forceful.

Conclusion

Facing the issues and conceptualizations outlined above will require new theological methodologies which we can only start to think of. As some of us have pointed out earlier,[21] we will need a combination of the conceptual and the narrative. While the secular women's movement in its attempt to analyse culture and religion could benefit from some of the hermeneutical debates on biblical texts, Christian feminists need to widen their perception of feminist social analysis in order even to locate themselves successfully in the first step of the hermeneutic circle. The spaces for intercultural sharing of women's faith and aspirations have to be opened up not only within church and theology but within the life world of daily interaction and in the day-to-day reality of women's survival struggles.

Notes

1. Kamla Bhasin and Nighat Said Khan, *Some Questions on Feminism and its Relevance in South Asia*, Kali for Women 1990.

2. Bina Agarwal, 'The Gender and Environment Debate: Lessons from India', *Feminist Studies* 18. 1, 1992, 119–55.

3. Ibid., 151.

4. Vandana Shiva, *Staying Alive*, Kali for Women 1988; Vandana Shiva and Maria Mies, *Ecofeminism*, London 1991.

5. Cecile Jackson, 'Radical Environmental Myths: A Gender Perspective', *New Left Review* 210, 124–40.

6. See her discussion paper submitted to RC 32 at the Bielefeldt International Sociology Congress, July 1994.

7. *Pressing Against the Boundaries*, Report FAO, New Delhi 1989, 54.

8. Vandana Shiva (ed.), *Minding our Bodies. Women from the South and North Reconnect Ecology and Health*, Kali for Women 1993.

9. 'Women and Religious Identities in India after Ayodhya', in *Against all Odds*, ed. Kamla Bhasin, Ritu Menon and Nighat Said Khan, Kali for Women 1994.

10. See Shiraz Sidhva, 'Dukhtaram-e-Millett: Profile of a Militant, Fundamentalist Women's Organization', in *Against All Odds* (n. 9), 123–31.

11. Paola Bacchetta, '"All our goddesses are armed", Religion, Resistance and Revenge in the Life of a Militant Hindu Nationalist Woman', in *Against all Odds* (n. 9), 153f.

12. Margaret Shanti and Corona Mary (eds.), *We Dare to Speak*, Worth Study Series 1, 1994.

13. Parita Mukta, *Upholding the Common Life. The Community of Mirabai*, London 1994, 91.

14. See Flavia's *My Story . . . Our Story of Rebuilding Broken Lives*, Bombay 1984.

15. See e.g. Madhu Kishwar's article, 'Safety is Indivisible. The Warming from Bombay Riots', and Flavia Agnes, 'Behrampada – A Besieged Basti', in *Manushi* 74–75, January-April 1993.

16. *The Broken Palmyra*, Claremont, CA 1990. See also John Merrit, 'The Battle for No Man's Land', *The Observer*, 29 April 1990, 46ff.

17. Gail Omvedt, *Violence Against Women. New Movements and New Theories in India*, Kali for Women 1990.

18. Vandana Shiva, *The Violence of the Green Revolution. Ecological Degradation and Political Conflict in Punjab*, Dehradun 1989.

19. Gabriele Dietrich, 'The World as the Body of God', *Journal of Dharma* XVIII.3, 1993.

20. Some of the conceptual framework used here is taken from the Frankfurt school of sociology and its discussion with systems theory. My colleague David Rajendran has applied some of this to Indian people's movements in his doctoral research. I draw partly on discussions with him.

21. See Margret Shanthi, 'Towards a Feminist Theology', and Gabriele Dietrich, 'On Doing Feminist Theology in South Asia', *Kristu Jyoti* 6.2, June 1990.

Eve's Knowing: Feminist Theology's Resistance to Malestream Epistemological Frameworks

Rebecca Chopp

In many traditional 'malestream' interpretations of Genesis, Eve's great fault was to want to know. Her fall into sin, from a Christian perspective, must be located in her desire to be an active agent and thus to risk entering the epistemological fray. Her willingness to partake of the fruit of the tree of knowledge, and the resulting deceptiveness that resulted from this act, from the beginning creates an uneasy relation of women and knowledge, at least as seen from a malestream epistemology.

Feminist interpreters of this biblical scripture point out that there are other ways to read this text. But whether or not the fearful alliance between women and epistemology is in the text or in the interpreters or in both, the fact remains that woman as epistemological agent, according to malestream epistemological frameworks, has been seen as not merely morally wrong, but dangerous.

So dangerous is this alliance of women and knowledge that the resolve was simple: separate women from epistemology. The historical and cultural conditions seemed, after all, 'naturally' to keep women at home, tied to childbirth and child-rearing. Women's smaller physical development, and thus 'smaller brain', also served to 'prove' that women could not be epistemological agents. The created order necessitated the inferior helpmate of man to be at home: protected under man's knowledge, woman could maintain her place in creation as helpmate.

Western epistemology and theology together developed the view that women were naturally more emotional and irrational, prone to hysteria and often quite childlike. A few modern theologians seem to depart from this patriarchal view. Schleiermacher's *Christmas Eve Dialogue* portrays women and their stories of Jesus as closer to fundamental religious affection than man's dry, abstract discourse. But still closer to Jesus, for Schleiermacher, was the girl Sophie's simple trust. Schleiermacher, and other exceptions, did not really challenge the necessary division between women and epistemology, but simply used it as a way to move religion outside the limits of modern epistemology.

Feminine theorists and theologians resist not only the 'dangerous' relation between women and knowledge, but the 'naturalness' of the identification of epistemology and the rights of men, at least a particular group of men. Feminists resist the dominant or 'malestream' epistemology as fashioned for the benefit of men. The term 'malestream' epistemology suggests two interrelated meanings. First of all, the dominant epistemo- logy tends to privilege white, European males by focussing on particular aspects of knowledge such as autonomy and objectivity. The underside of this statement is obvious: epistemology gets narrowed, and multiple ways of knowing are not allowed. Secondly, dominant epistemology tends to be gendered with knowledge (or the privileged aspects of knowledge) being identified as masculine, while the emotions and the body are gendered as feminine. A natural alliance is established between men and knowledge, while women assume the feminine position of the body and the emotions.

Feminist critique of malestream epistemology has to do with how a social construction of knowledge gets represented as 'natural', thus masking particular relations of interest, power and knowledge that benefit a particular group of males. Knowledge, according to feminist theologians, has not just been done *by* a particular group of men, but *for* a particular group of men. It has been to this group of men's advantage to perpetuate the 'natural' recognition that women, and persons of colour, are irrational, weak in the mind, too dependent, and incapable of abstract thought.

Feminist theologians argue that malestream epistemology is not the universal, abstract truth it claims to be. Rather, as an ideology, malestream epistemologies function to oppress and belittle those who are other than the white, privileged men in charge of knowledge. Malestream theologians trumpet their epistemology as based on pure, abstract reason, universal for all times and places, not dependent upon material conditions and not suspect to irrational, emotional claims. Feminist theologians contend that such epistemology uses this guise to construct theologies that privilege the experience of those who write such theology and serve to oppress those who, due to material conditions, do not share such privilege. Thus feminists argue that malestream epistemology suffers from ideological distortion. Ideology is not about individual intentional desire, but rather about how the 'common sense' structures that are beyond any one thinker become the location and the material for oppressive thought. For instance, the dearly held assumption that women are not as smart as men is not something to which each human comes out of empirical research. Rather, it is presented to us in the media when men are depicted as bankers, doctors and lawyers and women live off men, though they may do the unpaid domestic work of cleaning, cooking and rearing children.

One of the best-known essays in the critique of malestream epistemologies was Valerie Saiving's 'The Human Situation: A Feminine View'. Saiving recounted her experience of sitting in a doctoral class of theology and reading Reinhold Niebuhr and Anders Nygren on the universal declaration that sin has to do with self-assertion and love with selflessness. Saiving realized that Niebuhr and Nygren were basing their 'universal' interpretation on the experience of men. In the space cleared by her criticism, Saiving probed the nature of woman's experience as different from man's and the need for theology to reflect upon the experience of women. This small article stands as a gem of feminist ideology critique: men (a certain group of men) used their experience and called it universal, but it really wasn't the experience of women (or a group of women). Though feminist critique would itself have to learn to be resistant to any one notion of universal woman's experience, the logic remains the same: knowledge is reflective – consciously or unconsciously – of the speaker and his or her particular social location.

The theologians of malestream epistemology belonged to a class and a community very much in power in the West. The class found it beneficial to argue for a universal epistemology, where knowledge obeys the same rules everywhere and an epistemological knower that was at one and the same time abstract and autonomous. The feminist ideology critique of malestream epistemology has two basic, and interrelated, parts: a critique of the universalism of malestream epistemology and a critique of the privileging of an abstract, autonomous, knower.

Western epistemology has focussed on universal reason – the nature of knowledge as universal above the messiness of history. Knowledge, at least in Western modernity, gets constructed over against tradition and traditional authorities. Real knowledge is that which, in principle, is accessible to all persons at all times and places. This universal nature of epistemology, aside from concrete history, was spoken of in various structures of consciousness, of ontology, or of existentialism that exist behind or beyond all history. Such structures became ways to refer to God, so God was the ontological ground, the referent of consciousness, the contact point of existential structures.

The second aspect of the feminist ideology critique of malestream epistemologies has to do with the autonomy of the knower and the corresponding abstraction of modern knowledge. Knowledge, for the Cartesian subject, is located within the individual, in the structures of consciousness, in the ability of observation, or in the natural law or will within the individual. Theologians like Tillich could identify with great confidence a structure of existence as well as one of essence! And a category that dominated modern theological method was that of adequacy and credibility to common human experience. Common human experience was arrived at through abstract reflection, which relies on the ability of the knower to remove himself from history, emotions and the body. This individual may participate in community and society, but what guides his participation, hopefully at least, will be reason, that which rises above society, history and the body.

Such epistemological assumptions, according to feminist critiques, get projected upon the supreme knower: God. As wholly other, God is unaffected by time and space. As radically monotheistic, God is autonomous and abstract. God is the supreme Father and, as the popular American TV show of the 1950s suggested, Father knows best. Mary Daly, whose ideology critique in *Beyond God the Father* nearly turned theological epistemology inside out, suggested 'If God is male, then male is God.' Feminist critique of malestream epistemology uncovered the crucial link between the contours of modern epistemology and absoluteness of God: both were to be spoken of in language descriptive of the men in power in history.

Feminist resistance to malestream epistemology includes not only such critique but also the creation of viable alternative epistemologies. Feminist epistemological alternatives have developed in two basic responses: standpoint theory and social constructionism. Feminist standpoint theory contends that where you are positioned dictates the kind of knowledge you have. Women, so this epistemology holds, who have been positioned as other than men, have had to learn the ways of men but also the ways of women. This 'double consciousness' has allowed women not only a broader sense of knowledge but also a preferable sense of knowledge. The preferable sense of knowledge is because women's ways of knowing are often more valuable and more important. 'Women's ways of knowing', so to speak, offer an epistemic privilege. There can be a variety of forms of standpoint theory, from the position of Mary Daly, who argues that women's knowing is ontologically different from men's, to the position of more romantic feminist theologians, who will suggest that women essentially know more about loving, living, or even God. While standpoint theory is an easy correlate of ideology critique, its problems are insurmountable. Feminist standpoint epistemology assumes that all women are the same. This assumption of essentialism (all women are in essence the same) is often connected with the position of white middle-class first-world women who assume that women from other social locations will be like them. Feminist standpoint theory also just reverses a kind of epistemological dualism, giving value to whatever form of knowledge might be gendered as female.

In more recent years, feminist epistemology has increasingly become that of a social constructionist version. Social constructionism maintains that knowledge is itself always historical, always related to power and interests, and is open to change and transformation. Knowledge is crafted from past traditions, contemporary structures, and future possibilities. In the social constructionist version of feminist epistemology, knowledge is constructed from three primary sources or places: 1. tradition and texts; 2. experience; and 3. participation in social movements. These three are not necessarily antithetical, and many feminist theologians combine them in various ways. At the same time, most feminist theologians tend to construct epistemology primarily from one of these places, and then will draw upon the other two.

1. *Tradition and texts*. If knowledge is no longer to be situated within pure, abstract reason, one place we can locate knowledge is in cultural and religious traditions, and especially in the texts of those traditions. This version of social constructionism is influenced both by philosophical hermeneutics and by cultural anthropology. Because this version centres knowledge in texts of tradition, it builds easily upon the Christian predisposition to locate knowledge, especially revealed knowledge, in scripture and tradition. But since many of the dominant texts of the Christian tradition contain patriarchal orderings and sayings, feminists must counter this epistemological bias. Some counter the patriarchal leanings of the Christian tradition by arguing for a special strand of tradition that is the true tradition. Rosemary Radford Ruether, for instance, argues for the notion of a prophetic-liberatory tradition that opposes the patriarchal parts of tradition. Other feminists argue that the tradition contains its own critique of patriarchy. Elizabeth Johnson's *She Who Is* exemplifies this tradition-friendly response. Still other feminists expand the canon of tradition, finding texts written by women to be just as epistemologically privileged. Katie Cannon in *Black Womanist Ethics* turns to the work of Zora Neale Hurston, Howard Thurman and Martin Luther King, Jr, to create an ethic for black women from an expanded notion of canon.

2. *Reconstructing experience*. Feminist theologians have often wanted

to adhere to women's experience as a source of knowing. As in the standpoint theory of epistemology, it is often maintained that women's experience yields ways of knowing not available in malestream epistemology. And, as I have suggested, such a conclusion can lead to some insurmountable problems. Are all women's experiences the same? Are women's experiences just the opposite of, and even better than, men's experiences (the problem of dualism)? Yet just because we should not *essentialize* experience, there must be some way that experience itself can be epistemologically significant. Most religions, after all, do maintain some role for religious experience as a way of knowing the divine. The question is, then, in what way experience is epistemologically significant. Feminist theologians who explore this version of social constructionism tend to focus on the diversity of experience, the construction of experience in language itself, and the ongoing dialogue of different experiences. Susan Brooks Thistlethwaite in *Sex, Race, and God*, and Ida Maria Isiasi-Diaz in *En La Lucha*, provide two quite different ways of speaking of knowing in relation to diverse experiences.

3. *Participation in social movements*. The most openly constructionist version of epistemology is located among those feminists who tend to de-centre notions of epistemology and argue for the centrality of critical theory within a liberationist movement. A critical theory is the operation of knowledge of deliberation of beliefs and activities in a community. As such, critical theories seek to uncover illusions, such as the socially constructed belief that it is natural for men to be superior to women. Critical theories uncover how epistemological discourses construct regimes of domination: how the knowledge of men's natural superiority and women's naturally inferiority has functioned to justify the oppression, including the physical battering and rape, of women. As a substitute to the centrality of epistemology, a critical theory takes as its departure point the reality of oppression and suffering in society and attempts both to display the origin, function and relations of structures that cause such oppression and to anticipate possibilities for change. Involved in both critique and transformation, imagination becomes central to the nature of critical theory. Feminist theologians such as Elisabeth Schüssler Fiorenza and Rebecca S. Chopp advocate the decentring of epistemological questions for the primacy of critical theory.

As I have already mentioned, these three versions of social constructionist epistemology tend to overlap within most thinkers. It is important to see the distinctions of epistemological versions, because 'knowledge' has quite specific contours given a beginning in texts, or experience, or social movement. Still, by way of summary, we can also say that feminist theological epistemologies share two dominant strategies of resistance to and subversion of malestream epistemology. The first strategy of resistance/subversion is to deny the ahistorical character of epistemology that sets it apart from ethical concerns, and to locate knowledge in history and as always already connected with interests, power. In this strategy, knowledge, theory and reason become connected to ethics. The second strategy of resistance to and subversion of malestream epistemology is to expand broadly the definition of epistemology from abstract reason to multiple ways of knowing, including bodily, imaginative, dialogical and relational knowing.

The first strategy of resistance/subversion has to do with overcoming the malestream epistemological notion that knowledge, in order to be knowledge, must be removed from history, both in terms of the ideal knower and in terms of the very structure of reason. If malestream epistemology argues the importance of abstracting from history, feminist theologies join contemporary critics in the insistence of knowing through history. Two claims are involved here. First, the reality of knowledge is that we know through history – we are both determined by the limits of historical knowledge and at the same time are provided with possibilities through that knowledge. Knowledge is always constructed in and through historical, communal traditions. Since knowledge is always historical, epistemology must always take upon itself the ethical responsibility of its form and effect. Since interest and power are linked to knowledge, the epistemological task is also always an ethical task: who benefits from this knowledge? Feminist theologians insist both on the importance of drawing knowledge through experience and the social location of any experience. So knowledge is not universal, nor is it from the autonomous knower. Knowledge is in and through our social, communal situatedness.

The second strategy of resistance/subversion has to do with the broad expansion of what gets counted as 'knowledge'. In malestream epistemology what counts as knowledge has to do with abstract structures, and knowledge is narrowed to a particular form of rational cognition limited to linguistic and logical-mathematical ordering. Feminist theologies oppose the narrow limiting of epistemology. Feminist epistemology seeks to broaden knowledge through relational knowing, embodied knowing, intuitive knowing, imaginative knowing. To know God is not only to argue or analyse the referent of God through or at the limit of human existence. We know God through communal practices, through physical experiences, through the soaring imaginings of the mind. Sites of knowledge may be art, liturgy or relationships as well as texts, discursive arguments and theological debates.

Eve's knowing, feminists may well argue, was threatening to malestream epistemology. Eve was dangerous because she would uncover the knower for his own hubris and control. Her danger exists not only in her act of uncovering but also in the expansiveness of her knowing. The fruit, so to speak, of Eve's agency would be the ambiguities, and yet the possibilities, of many ways of knowing.

Bibliography

Katie Cannon, *Black Womanist Ethics*, Atlanta 1988.

Rebecca S. Chopp, *Saving Work: Feminist Practices of Theological Education*, Louisville, Ky 1995.

Ada Maria Isasi-Diaz, *En la Lucha, In the Struggle: A Hispanic Women's Liberation Theology*, Minneapolis 1993.

Elisabeth Schüssler Fiorenza, *But She Said: Feminist Practices of Biblical Interpretation*, Boston 1992.

Elizabeth A. Johnson, *She Who Is: The Mystery of God in Feminist Theological Discourse*, New York 1992.

Rosemary Radford Ruether, *Sexism and God-Talk: Toward a Feminist Theology*, Boston and London 1983.

Valerie Saiving, 'The Human Situation: A Feminine View', in *Womanspirit Rising: A Feminist Reader in Religion*, ed. Carol Christ and Judith Plaskow, San Francisco 1970.

Susan Brooks Thistlethwaite, *Sex, Race, and God: Christian Feminism in Black and White*, New York 1989.

Thought about Sexual Difference and Theology: The Italian Debate

Elizabeth E. Green

For some years now in Italy, conditions have been in the making for the development of a truly indigenous feminist theology. So far, the few theological attempts to combine theological thought and feminist theory have been inspired above all by feminist theology from abroad, and we have tried to translate or transplant the concepts used in them for a country which is not always receptive. Without denying this heritage, which for many of us remains fundamental, women theologians are now seeking more our own philosophy of sexual difference, the result of the work of some of the women's movement in Italy.

Thus work is going on in Italy, on feminist theory and confessional theologies and various disciplines, which is advancing theological reflection on the feminine. Throughout the country a dialogue is beginning between women theologians and philosophers, which is wanted by both sides. For example, the philosopher Adriana Cavarero has addressed a clear invitation to theologians, with reference to Genesis 1.27, to 'think about the original duality in its unexpressed possibilities',[1] while the theologian M. Cristina Bartolomei defines thought about sexual difference 'as a question which goes back to the beginning and which relates to everything', i.e. as 'a major question of theology'.[2] Furthermore, the same thinking about this difference has not been unaware of the thought of theologians from the United States like Mary Daly, Rosemary Ruether and Elisabeth Schüssler Fiorenza.

In this article I therefore propose to describe some theological features which are emerging in Italy in connection with reflection on the difference between the sexes. First, I shall indicate the premises of this thought; then, I shall describe its approach to the divine; thirdly, I shall show how Italian theology is orientating itself in this connection;

and finally, I shall consider the nature of the two discourses involved in the dialogue.

I The premises of thought about sexual difference

The thought about sexual difference which interests me in this analysis has been developed by Diotima, a philosophical community of women which was founded in 1983; its points of reference include the work of Luce Irigaray, the French philosopher, linguist and psycho-analyst. Diotima has in fact done everything possible to translate and disseminate Irigaray's thought in Italy, to such a degree that Luisa Muraro has been able to say: 'There is no country in Europe, including France, in which Irigaray is better known and regarded.'[3] Furthermore, Muraro, the linchpin of Diotima, recognizes that it was the writings of Irigaray which provided 'the authorization to use theological language in the work of bringing female experience to expression'.[4]

Among the premises of such thought, mention should first be made of the importance of symbolism, i.e. the capacity of women to give names to reality, to interpret it. According to this way of thinking, our freedom takes place particularly at the symbolic level, that is, in the way in which we perceive both ourselves and the world, or what Anglo-Saxon women have called 'the power of naming'. To give priority to the symbolic order does not mean being uninterested in the real conditions in which women live, since given the close relationship between the symbolic order and the social order, 'the interpretation of the world is part of the transformation of the world'.[5]

Secondly, there is the awareness that the interpretation of the world given by philosophy (or theology) is the work of a male subject who, simply by giving names to reality on the basis of his particular sexuality, is erected *(sic)* as the neutral universal subject. Claiming the right to speak for women as well, men have in effect excluded women from discourse, in that 'female experience . . . is deprived of any possibility of a meaning for itself'.[6]

Thirdly, 'human nature is twofold'.[7] Every human being is of either the male or the female sex, and therefore neither the one nor the other can express the totality of the human species. This simple fact, evident to anyone, without which the world would not go on, has not been reflected upon, 'with the result that no significance has been attached to the presence of sexual difference'.[8]

II The difference and the divine

Two aspects of the complex and not always homogeneous discourse of reflection on sexual difference have proved of particular interest to women theologians. The first is the divinization of the feminine gender, and the second is the figure of the mother as the source of the symbolic competence of women.

According to Irigaray's well-known essay on 'Divine Women', developed in Italy by A. Buttarelli,[9] women can only give meaning to their sexual particularity, their feminine nature, within a horizon of transcendence. In other words, individual finitude cannot exist without an infinite which relates to the real, making us aware of our limits. For Feuerbach, by whom this author is influenced, the figure of God was the result of a human projection of attributes of the male sex; it served to orientate individuals in their becoming. However, the values and aspirations of the female gender are excluded by this God, so that women have been deprived of the possibility of realizing themselves by 'not becoming male'. What is lacking in the possibility of women's development is a female God who on the one hand allows women to transcend themselves, and on the other stands as a limit to this transcendence. For women to be able to affirm and realize themselves it is therefore vital to name a God in the feminine, to create, if one wants to put it that way, a God in our image and likeness. Only if God can become incarnate in the feminine, Irigaray affirms, can women become divine.

Luisa Muraro also sets out to liberate for women the positions which have been occupied by the male God and his surrogates (father, husband, son, pope, parish priest), thus preventing women from interpreting the real. However, Muraro does not propose to replace the male God with a female God but with the real mother. In fact, it is the mother (and not the father) who gives her son or daughter both reality (through her body) and the capacity to interpret it (by means of the word): 'Being (or having) a body and being (or having) a word develop together . . . and the work of the mother consists specifically in this togetherness.'[10] Thus in order to create a symbolic feminine order, women have to reconcile themselves with the mother. It is true, Muraro maintains, that to create symbolic order the mother allows her place to be taken by others, including God, but in the last analysis these substitutions serve to restore the mother. Women like Wilhelmina of Bohemia, Teresa of Avila and Simone Weil, who for thought about sexual difference are examples of freedom, can help in this undertaking. Although these figures had a direct relationship with the transcendent – without any male intermediaries – they serve not to point towards the divine but to reconcile us with the real mother. Not only our symbolic competence but also the capacity to recognize the authority of the other derives from this reconciliation. In this way, thought about sexual difference also seeks to express the inequality among women.

Thus two proposals arise from thought about sexual difference, one about the divinization of the female gender and the other about the mother as foundation of a symbolic feminine order. These two lines, which tend to get entangled in the women – often mystics – most emphasized in the female genealogy of Diotima, are even more interwoven in theological reflection.

III Feminist theology and thought about sexual difference

The project of thought about sexual difference which seeks to express the feminine element in the divine comes close to one of the aims which feminist theology has had from the beginning, namely a quest for feminine images of God. How are Italian women theologians beginning to measure up to the concerns about the divine feminine which emerge from thought about sexual difference?

One proposal goes in the direction of the divinization of Mary. Starting with her experience that the only divine element that can be recognized in everyday life is a woman, because God appears too unattainable, Ivana Ceresa proposes to take over all the Marian dogmas, beginning with the *theotokos*, in order to make Mary an independent divine figure. It is primarily the motherhood of Mary which attracts Ceresa's attention; the fact that men have come to give the title 'Mother of God' to Mary deserves careful reflection on the part of women. In fact Ceresa proposes to regard Mary as the 'woman whom God has become, in order to think of God's self as human'.[11] Thus this author seeks to detach Mary from the Christ to bring her near to the Spirit, of which we cannot exclude the possibility that she is an incarnation.

In a country like Italy, in which confessionalism still plays a basic role in theology, it is clear, as the Protestant Letizia Tomassone affirms in connection with Mary, that 'it is more a question of where one stands'.[12] There is no doubt that the Madonna has 'a symbolic connotation which calls for a complete re-reading', but is it not also true, as Ceresa maintains, that 'we have nothing to fear from mariology'?[13] The debate is open, but the positive reading of Boff's mariology by Ceresa seems to me a small alarm signal about the implications of this proposal. In fact Boff puts forward an androgynous model which has been rejected by feminist theology, and does not entirely succeed in avoiding the complementarity between the sexes which is rejected by thought about sexual difference.[14]

Cettina Militello, a lecturer in mariology, makes a basic objection to this line and to the Feuerbachian thesis adopted by Diotima: 'the more concessions are made to woman on an ideal level, the more she is humiliated on a real level'.[15] In other words, thought about sexual difference would end up by imposing the old stereotypes of female patriarchy. On the one hand, Militello argues that Mary is still used to identify woman with maternity or with her biological particularity. On the other hand, she argues that the femininization of the Spirit and the emphasis on mysticism ends up by identifying women with an illogical language, denying them the capacity of reasoning. Finally, in clear contrast to thought about sexual difference, Militello does not want to deprive men of the rich symbolism which Mary offers them: 'Does not the appeal to the archetypal feminity of the Mother of God perhaps deprive the whole of humanity, men and women, of their model in the realm of faith and discipleship?'[16]

In these theologians we find two contrasting positions. Ceresa emphasizes Irigary's reading of Feuerbach ('someone who has become more woman and less God is a male')[17] which Militello rejects. For Ceresa, thought about sexual difference provides a key for reading the perpetual virginity of Mary, the Immaculate Conception and the Assumption, which seeks to make Mary an incarnation of the feminine element of the divine for women. Will this interpretative ploy (based in part on the perception that women already have of the Madonna) succeed in making Mary a source of feminine freedom, or will it end up, as Militello argues, restricting women to motherhood (under the complacent gaze of a male church)? In opposition to thought about sexual difference, Militello chooses a different interpretative strategy: as women are 'included' in the sexual partiality of the Son, so men are 'included' in the sexual particularity of Mary. If, thanks to the Son, women are 'also' included in the incarnation, thanks to Mary men can 'also' form part of perfect humanity. But only when there is an emphasis on the emancipating thread of mariology is there a need to accept that yet again we have that scheme by which the male is thought suited to symbolize the divine while the female can only and always decline the human.

Thus in dialogue with thought about sexual difference, Ceresa proposes to use traditional mariology to get beyond its limits, projecting the feminine on to God, while Militello argues that such a manoeuvre identifies women with their bodies and deprives them of the Logos. Wanting to speak of God in the feminine but at the same time wanting to claim the authority of the Logos for women, I have used thought about sexual difference to decline the divine word in the feminine.

We have seen that for Muraro, in fact language is not the gift of the father (who introduces the child to symbolism at the cost of separating it from the mother), but of the mother, who unites in herself word and body. While

Christianity has always declined the relationship between the word and reality in the three moments of creation, incarnation and regeneration, in the masculine (by means of the Logos), this relationship can be expressed in the feminine, by means of Sophia – thanks to a correlation between thought about sexual difference and the wisdom tradition in scripture. So it is a matter of reading the theological and christological tradition backwards, discounting the masculinization of Sophia and daring, through Sophia, a feminization of both God and Christ.

In this reading, God, read through Sophia, takes the place of the real mother, whom Muraro sees as the foundation of the feminine symbolic order. The genealogy of women in the Bible can help to get back to this God. An in-depth study of the saga about women in II Samuel, for example, shows that their symbolic competence was capable of transforming reality. Their authority was not only maternal in origin but was also the fruit of a different understanding of God which later the tradition declined explicitly in the feminine.[18]

However, an awareness remains among women theologians that the feminization of God, although it seems to me to be necessary, is not sufficient. It is a stage in the process of the de-masculinization of God, the end of which still remains for some women the de-sexualization of God. This de-sexualization is open to different interpretations. Tomassone argues against a substitution pure and simple of God the Father with a mother God. There is a need to 'change the structure of God' and recover, along the lines of Eckart and Tillich, a God beyond God, who puts in question any image of the divine.[19] For Militello, desexualization means basing the reciprocity on which the whole of her thought turns not – like Boff – on the two sexual forms together but on the trinitarian relationships.[20] Thought about sexual difference for which desexualization does not exist proves very perplexed at this theological proposal; this reaction is a sign of the distance which separates the two projects, a distance which makes itself felt despite the mutual enrichment between theology and philosophy.

IV A common language, different discourses?

It is not an easy undertaking to identify the precise meaning of the word 'God' or similar concepts like 'divine' or 'transcendence' in the various writings about sexual difference. In reading the texts of Irigaray, for example, Muraro interprets 'God' as 'feminine freedom'. She points out: 'I do not know how much God interests me, whereas I am very interested in women's freedom, and the magnitude of this interest leads me, among other things, to be preoccupied with God, because I think that this can be useful.'[21] Such an interpretation does not seem to me to be illegitimate while the divine remains, according to the thesis of Feuerbach adopted by Irigaray and others, a symbolic construction which helps women to realize themselves. Furthermore Muraro guards against the temptation to put God in the place of the mother, arguing that we know very little about the way in which God 'would restore an original perspective to women . . . , while we know a good deal, a very great deal, about the way in which he restores it to men'.[22] Although Muraro considers the undertaking hazardous, in that God and the masculine are too much tangled up together, as a theologian I at any rate have sought to build on this 'very little' through reflection on sexual difference, in order to bring the 'more' to light. In this sense it can be said that women theologians are committed in their theologizing, or perhaps better re-theologizing, to a laicized religious discourse. Concepts from a Christian framework like recognition, gratitude and trust, used in thinking about sexual difference with reference to the mother or to other women, are therefore taken up by women theologians to talk of relations with God.

On the other hand, however, the tendency to confuse women's freedom with God is not absent from theology which is more open to thought about difference. The risk that this theology runs is that of reducing the reality of God to women's freedom. At this point, paradoxically, it is Muraro herself who speaks out against the laicization of transcendence and is preoccupied along with her other colleagues in Diotima, with a feminine genealogy in which women appear with a keen sense not only of the divine, but of God.

The women theologians who enter into dialogue with thought about sexual difference therefore encounter a discourse which is already pregnant with religious meaning, though its status remains ambiguous. Although both forms of discourse link God with women's freedom, they do so from different perspectives and with distinct emphases. If thought about sexual difference reflects on the divinization of the female gender, theology puts forward, rather, the feminization of God. If thought about sexual difference uses religious language to talk about the real mother, theology takes over Diotima's language about the mother to talk of God.

Sometimes the common language conceals the difference between the two discourses. At other times such diversity is explicit, in both philosophy and theology. For example, although Muraro feels close to women who work for women's freedom in their own church, she clearly asserts that it is now too late for Christianity to become a religion of such freedom.[23] On the other hand, the Protestant Spano, while regarding thought about sexual difference as a useful instrument with which theology can express the salvation which comes from outside us, notes that in this thought 'the soteriological and symbolic levels tend to become identified'.[24]

In this article, I have presented some of the tendencies which are emerging in Italy from the dialogue between a philosophy of sexual difference and a feminist theology. In her book *Dissonanze*, Rosy Braidotti calls on us to waste no more time in senseless comparisons between feminism of French origin and that with an Anglo-Saxon stamp.[25] Similarly, I am convinced that the debate in Italy can only benefit from a broader encounter with feminist theology, but I am also convinced that feminist theology has everything to gain if it pays attention to the fertile debate which is taking place in Italy between theology and thought about sexual difference.

Translated by Mortimer Bear

Notes

1. Adriano Cavarero, 'Per una teoria della differenza sessuale', in Diotima, *Il pensiero della differenza sessuale*, Milan 1989, 70.
2. M. C. Bartolomei, *Progetto Donna* 2–3, 1989, 10, quoted by M. Grazie Fasoli, 'Donne e teologia', in *Gli specchi delle donne*, Milan 1994, 18.
3. Franca Bezzi and Letizia Tomassone, 'Intervista a Luisa Muraro', *Gioventù Evangelica* 41, 1991, 13.
4. Luisa Muraro, 'La nostra comune capacità di infinito', in Diotima, *Mettere al mondo il mondo*, Milan 1990, 74.
5. L. Muraro, *Tre lezioni sulla differenza sessuale*, Rome 1994, 73.
6. L. Muraro, *L'ordine simbolico della madre*, Rome 1991, 79.
7. Luce Irigaray, *Amo a te*, Turin 1993, 42–9.
8. Cavarero, 'Per una teoria' (n. 1), 77.
9. L. Irigaray, 'Donne divine', in *Sessi e genealogie*, Milan 1989, 67–86; Annarosa Buttarelli, 'Dio personale e genere femminile', in Ivana Ceresa (ed.), *Donne e divino*, Mantua 1992, 44–50.
10. Muraro, *Ordine simbolico* (n. 6), 126.
11. Ibid., 40.
12. 'Il paradosso della libertà', *Quaderni di Agape* 24, 1994, 35.
13. Ibid., 17.
14. Leonardo Boff, *Il volto materno di Dio*, Brescia 1981.
15. C. Militello, *Donna in questione*, Assisi 1992.
16. Ibid., 160.
17. Ibid., 40.
18. Elizabeth Green, 'Parole di donne', in *Filosofia donne filosofie*, Lecce 1994, 313–22; 'Donne sagge', *Rivista biblica*, 1996.
19. Ceresa, 'La trascendenza nella teologia cristiana classica e femminista', in Ceresa, *Donne e divino* (n. 9), 114.
20. Ibid., 247ff.

21. Bezzi, 'Intervista' (n. 4), 17.
22. Muraro, *L'ordino simbolico* (n. 6), 53.
23. Muraro, 'La libertà femminile alleata con dio', *Gioventù Evangelica* 41. 127, 1991, 31.
24. Francesca Spano, 'Tra emancipazione e libertà femminile', *Gioventù Evangelica* 44. 142/3, 1993, 30.
25. R. Braidotti, *Dissonanze*, Milan 1994, 251.

The Indecency of Her Teaching: Notes for a *Cuceb* Teaching of Feminist Theology in Europe

Marcella Althaus-Reid

Cuceb means Revolution,
Literally speaking 'squirrel' (which turns round).
Then will be the end of begging and covetousness.[1]

(Ernesto Cardenal)

The Maya people of Latin America used the word *cuceb* for what we today can roughly translate as revolution. *Cuceb* literally means 'a squirrel', and as such is a symbol of social changes and fast changes of direction, sometimes difficult to predict. Also, perhaps, the movements of a squirrel are a metaphor for the historical inevitability of such changes.

Teaching theology as part of a process of doing theology, is also a *cuceb*. It is only when teaching theology loses the sense of movement and urgency which comes with the changes in our historical time that we no longer do theology as part of an inevitable, daring praxis of social transformation. In this case, instead of teaching theology we teach the history of ideas, but deprived of their concreteness, that is, of the material circumstances which gave birth to them in the first place. It is by living and relating our experiences to a discourse about God that a genuine teaching, integrating action and reflection, can occur. The 'end of begging and covetousness' that Cardenal speaks of waits for our praxis, not our approval or justification of a theological orthodoxy which no longer relates to our lives.

Military expeditions versus living theology

As a Third World theologian teaching in Europe, my main preoccupation has always been how to do a theology which would not simply be an anabasic work, that is, a sort of military expedition characterized by its upward direction, from the coast to the interior of the country. I deliberately use a military metaphor because it explains the whole ethos of the process of current teaching of theology I want to avoid. Military training implies a process of discipline and homogenization, without space for dissent from the hegemonic ideology supporting the teaching. It also implies a banking system of theological education which ignores the actual experience of the students and the relevant issues of the community of students that should be a fundamental part of their own process of doing theology. After all, how do theologians become theologians if not by doing theology? The methodological question here is concerned with the domestication of students to do a right orthodoxy in theology, instead of a genuine orthopraxis.

However, the geography of our doing theology in the European academia is of a more complex nature. If we try to bring a way of doing theology from the coast, that is, from the periphery of the First World to the centre, as an extra subject in our curricula, teaching some exotic product such a feminist liberation theology, womanist or mujerista theology, then our possibilities are limited. The challenge for Third World women theologians in Europe is *to do* a Third World feminist theology on this continent, with the issues and the challenges of the society in which we are living.

This way of doing and teaching theology will make obsolete the current alienation between academia and the community, and between feminist theology as research and the daily life of the women in our cities. At the heart of this process, what we will be doing is redefining what theology is, who is the theologian and her role in her society. Apart from doing an integral theology with our students and community, we will be teaching to the new generations of women in our churches that there is more to being a theologian than titles, publications and jobs in the university. Being a theologian is a prophetic vocation, and nobody is a theologian on her own, but only in community. We need to *do* theology by *being* community, and by participating in the work of women's movements.

A 'full-stop' theology

Gustavo Gutiérrez has said that when we talk about 'liberation theologians', it needs to be clear that we are talking about: '*theologians*.

Full stop.'² We must avoid the ghettoization of theologies. Feminist theology is theology: full stop. It is a theology with a clear option in the subject of its reflection, women. For some of us, it is also an option for doing theology with poor women, wherever we are, in Latin America or in Europe, because poverty is defined not only in economic terms but in relation to the lack of control over their lives and the marginalization from the socio-economic policies that women suffer in their countries.

Feminist theology as a way of teaching

Feminist theology can also be defined as a particular way of teaching and doing theology which, with its concreteness of reflection, challenges any other theological teaching done from orthodoxy and not from orthopraxis. The materiality of Feminist Theology is the *cuceb*, and the ferment of many revolutions that need to be born out of women's critical thinking and action. The question is, how can the *cuceb*, the revolutionary squirrel, become the method and the content of our teaching within academia? Which theological categories should we use for this process? Can the academy become a community, or should we mediate between both? This last question is particularly acute in Britain, where historically university and community work are thought incompatible and theologians are classified into 'lay', 'ordained', 'academic' or 'experiential'. As a reflection of a classist society, life and theology seem to be made up of watertight compartments, with very little relation amongst them.

The issue, then, is the poverty of our theology. With few exceptions, the structures of the churches do not engage in a praxis from the poor at the grass-roots level, and the universities have a system which discourages any type of dialogue except with fellow theologians. The community of theologians reflecting together does not always exist as such, and feminist theologians, divided into different, sometimes bitterly disagreeing, factions do not have the discipline to gather together with the women of their communities, to think God through the poverty trap, the cuts in welfare benefits, increasing unemployment and the failure of our democratic system. The structures of sin of this sharply divided rich/poor society discourage solidarity, generosity and the work that feminist visionaries need to do to be a movement of change. We are living in a society surrounded by the begging and covetousness of which Cardenal wrote. What is our role as theologians here?

Cuceb as a method and content

The dialectics of decency/indecency is a feminist theological category that I have been using as a framework of understanding in my own work as a lecturer and a theologian involved with local communities. It comes from my own context and experience of life in my home country, Argentina, and it is especially useful in relation to the spatial division which is crucial in the process of alienation which is a woman's life.

The division of spaces in Latin American women's lives is more pronounced than in Europe, and manifested through the exaggeration of the symbolic dis-location of femininity, that is, between the normality (decency) of closed locations (houses) and eccentric placements (margins of the economic activity). It is precisely because of the exaggeration of this dialectic that it is relevant in particular situations of fragmentation, such as materialist feminist theologians teaching in the universities in the West.

Decency is a category brought to Latin America by the Conquistadors in the sixteenth century. It is closely related to the objectification of women as property through the institution of colonial marriage, the exaltation of reproduction amongst the white, foreign elite under a judicial superstructure committed to inheritance laws, and also to the confinement of women in certain legal (although the word used is 'decent') physical, emotional and economic spaces. A style of hair, certain colours of clothes, even the regulation of time in the sense of what women can or cannot do according to their ages, the time of the day or season, was essential in the ideological apparatus constructed to control women. However, poor women who worked and challenged the spatial limitations by choice or because they were inapplicable in their lives, conformed to the rule of indecency. Thus, decency as a theological category applies to the politics of what is considered proper, and the orderly state of things, in our lives as women and in our relation with God.

Indecency is, on the contrary, the *cuceb*, the reality of our experience which does not match and cannot validate the faith as ideology in which we have been brought up. Indecency is subversive, and it is interesting to notice how under dictatorial regimes such as that in Argentina during the 1970s, the imposed oppressive social order had an alliance with the definition of morality which is 'decency'. Women in the guerrilla forces were portrayed as immoral (promiscuous, in men's roles) in the same way that *fabriqueras* (women factory workers) were considered indecent ('loose' – out of control? – women, sexually available). The category of decency is so related to class and economic power that I have come to the conclusion that whenever there is a definition of 'decency' in my society, poor women are marginalized.

The need for indecency in our teaching

Could it be that our teaching in academia has become so decent, so respectable, that feminist theology is already becoming domesticated and as such, inefficacious? If theology is a *cuceb*, its teaching must be indecent by definition.

The first point to consider is geographical. In general, we are teaching in confined spaces which, depending on the institution, have alliances with a certain class ideology. In Britain, for instance, there is a privatization of theology, manifested by an emphasis on private sins and privately defined conflicts and solutions. People's sufferings have been privatized. Domestic violence has become 'private', geographically defined by a house; feminist theology needs to challenge this situation not only from the historical political experience of women, but by the use of mediator sciences which will help us to understand the situation of women in our societies. Our teaching should be part of an interdisciplinary process, integrating sociology, anthropology and economics.

The teacher then starts to work in a less private way. The theological issues, coming from the newspapers, are the ones which relate to life in the country and the circumstances of the life of the poorest of the poor in the whole world, women. The 'issue-based' approach to teaching encourages students to do theology, not as individuals, but as a group, and to feel empowered in their own situations. As Paulo Freire says, the teacher needs to be 'killed' by the students;[3] that is, she should be involved in a process of transferring authority to the students. The feminist theologian should challenge the decency of power and control over students which is so evident sometimes in the West, where students are not encouraged to participate actively in their own process of education.

However, it is not simply a case of changing our teaching in order to change the world, because both things need to happen simultaneously. The present structures in which we are working in the West do not necessarily consider the political participation of the lecturer in community work. In fact, in the interests of impartial detachment it is positively discouraged. When I started my first degree in theology in ISEDET, Buenos Aires, I went to work in a base community as part of the academic curriculum of the seminary. Moreover, leading theologians of liberation were doing the same sort of work, and Bonhoeffer's *Ethics* was discussed around the real, serious issues of the society in which we were living. The structures which do not allow this type of integrated curriculum have a clear option towards indifference and compliance, because theology cannot be done outside the world. These are structures of sin which work by fragmenting lives. The collective utopia of the *basileia* of God requires us to work together upon the symbolic and mythical universe of a nation, unmasking oppressive faith as ideology, and finding in the concreteness of our daily struggles a systematic theology that is not simply a heavy old monument that is to be preserved.

The teaching of feminist theology should provide this critical thinking and *poiesis*. As Juan Luis Segundo has said, to do theology now is not to justify the monuments of the past. It is to do everything again.[4] Not only ideology but utopia depends on this collective process. The indecency of it consists in the disrespect for fragmentation, for instance, in the false divisions between academic and experiential theologians, and also in the emphasis on the authority of the believers (as the community of reference of our teaching/doing theology). We have the responsibility to teach theology while criticizing the ideology behind it. However, the structures in which we are working in the West are powerful and domesticating in the extreme. The *cuceb* needs strategies, and the creation of counter-structures, too.

First of all, we need to reply to the question of community. Where do we find a community? I believe that unless we are related to a group of people in a process of action/reflection outside the universities, our feminist theology runs the risk of becoming essentialist and ineffective. The theologian needs her community base. It could be related to her particular struggle, violence against women, or women and jobs, but it could also be an ecumenical project. Part of the ethos of our fragmented society is manifested in the way in which we always try to start new projects, instead of supporting existing ones. The creation of a movement is vital. A movement provides us with several things:

1. The possibility of organizing flexible structures of community work according to need, and disposing of them when obsolete, while retaining a feeling of continuation.

2. The ability to be in tune with the *kairos* in its different facets and challenges, working at different levels but with a feeling of unity.

3. The teaching of a new understanding of the role of the feminist theologian; the rediscovery of her prophetic vocation for transformation, supported by other people who do not objectify her in relation to patriarchal categories of importance.

4. Basic support and encouragement from women sharing the same 'indecent' visions, avoiding fragmentation through work done in solidarity.

The ex-centricity of our teaching

The work of doing feminist theology at the margins is related to the ex-centricity of our doing theology. We challenge the 'centre core' of traditional theology in its sexist anthropology, and we exercise a permanent suspicion of the churches' ideological constructions of faith. Working in a poor council estate in Dundee, Scotland, co-ordinating a conscientization programme, I learned that the corpo-reality of feminist theology comes into life and 'leaves the books' when we observe the queues of women with children waiting for the local post office to open to cash their giros. This is the body language of the poor women, living at the geographical margins of the cities. They are women of suffering, but also have a great capacity for solidarity, resilience in the struggle against violence and deprivation, and an immense talent for organizing themselves for their children's welfare or whatever they feel could give them a more dignified life. With some of those women we 'read the Scriptures' while walking in the little shopping centre in the afternoon, when the wind swept along the empty beer cans and discarded bags of French fries and the graffiti seemed to be the only thing alive in the area. The gigantic poster of a washing powder brand helped us to talk about cleansing, and guilt, and what could be the meaning of 'redemption' and 'cleansing from sin', in a context of the patriarchal fear of menstruation.

Rosie Braidotti wrote that in any feminist philosophical enterprise we must first of all set ourselves the task of finding the female *cogito*. Thus she said that, 'We authorize for ourselves the statement: I/woman/think/as woman/therefore I am.'[5]

Although the acknowledgement of our individualities is crucial in feminist theology, we must not forget the words of Segundo: 'We need not carry any more the burden of a theology which leaves us alone at the moment of eating or praying. Do "pure thoughts" eat? Or does "pure" materia pray?'[6] Our women's *cogito* cannot be understood from the presupposition that individual existence is the thought and consciousness of our existence. This would imply that to exist is to think, and therefore consciousness is the real home of meaning. The body of Western theology rests on this pillar. However, the home of meaning is social praxis, because right actions are the foundation of speech. Moreover, the 'I' who wants to know is in reality a 'we', and feminist theology, done with a clear option for poor women, can even go further and say that the community of poor women are the *Da* of *Dasein*, who unmask the individualistic ego constructed by Western thought. As feminist theologians, our teaching/doing theology is *cuceb* when we help this process of naming our being from the poorest women in our communities, that is, incorporating in the process that which has been left aside: the otherness of the poor, or black, or lesbian, or the stranger amongst us, without whom we cannot become human. The teaching of feminist theology is essentially ontological and collective. To work in academia and in the struggle at the same time is the only possibility of fulfilling this task.

At the present moment, considering the structures of fragmentation in which we work, any curriculum which can incorporate a *cuceb* feminist theology runs the risk of being seen as 'indecent'. Our teaching/doing theology is composed of subversive strategies of survival and conscientization at different levels and scale. It is only through the construction of a movement and the obstinacy to fulfil our prophetic vocation in the re-creation amongst us of structures of support (because the struggle is bigger and more important than us), that we can start to find alternatives, starting with a new definition and value of ourselves as theologians. As Cardenal wrote in one of his poems:

What sort of stele are we going to carve out?
My duty is to be an interpreter.
Your duty (and mine)
is to be born once more.[7]

Indecent teachers from the Third World in Europe need to be reborn once more into a different context. All feminist theologians need to be born once more, in the act of a movement towards a genuine collective teaching/doing of our lives in a reflection in the light of the sacred.

Notes

1. Ernesto Cardenal, 'Ardilla de los tunes de un katún', *Nueva Antologia Poética*, Buenos Aires 1978.
2. From a seminar given by G. Gutiérrez in Stirling University, Scotland, March 1995.
3. Cf. P. Freire, in P. Freire and I. Shor, *A Pedagogy for Liberation*, London 1987, 89.
4. Cf. J. L. Segundo, *Qu'est-ce qu'un dogme? Liberté évangélique et vérité normative*, Paris 1992.
5. Quoted by P. Bono and S. Kemp (eds.), *Italian Feminist Thought. A Reader*, Oxford 1991, 17.
6. Cf. J. L. Segundo, *Existencialismo, Filosofia y Poesia*, Buenos Aires 1984, 8.
7. Ernesto Cardenal, '8 Ahau', *Nueva Antologia Poética* (n. 1).

Difference as a Category in Critical Theologies for the Liberation of Women

M. Shawn Copeland

By now, it is neither controversial nor polemical to state that the thorough-going critical hermeneutical, epistemological and praxial commitment of theology to the radical liberation of women insinuates a major pardigm shift in reflection on religion and its role and significance in various geographic, social (i.e. political, economic and technological) and cultural sectors. On the one hand, since these theologies are concerned with much more than the domination of women by men, they liberate reflection on religion, advance its criticality and vitality, restore its seriousness and authority. These critical theologies, whether they stem from the experiences of Aboriginal, African, Asian, Caribbean, European, Indian, Latin American, North American, Pacific Basin subjects, entail certain common fundamentals: women's experiences form the point of departure, ideology critique as well as critique of all forms of patriarchy, explicit identifiction of hermeneutical location, social analysis and praxial resistance to kyriarchal oppressions. Moreover, these theologies overcome the aleatory distantiations of modernity – secular from sacred, private from public, objectivity from subjectivity, thought from feeling, theory from praxis. They expose the elaborate prevarications that mask the massive atrocities that have come to define the last five hundred years of human history. On the other hand, these theologies resist reductive, levelling, binary or totalizing world views or systems that purport to impose any utopian solution to the maintenance and transmission of religious and societal oppression. These critical theologies instigate the emancipation of women's subjugated and violated bodies and knowledges; discredit reified and hegemonic ontological signifiers;

interrogate and engage common and different religious, social and theoretical sites of struggle.

These critical theologies affirm black, brown, red, yellow, white women in all their diversities, histories and cultures, even as they problematize those diversities, histories and cultures as well as those interconnecting cognitive, moral, religious, social praxial relations among and between these women at all points and in all sites of struggle. As the exercise of rationality in theology, such interrogation, engagement and problematization is extended through the notion of *difference*, which has increasingly displaced the notion of *sisterhood* as a key theoretical tool in critical feminist theologies.

For nearly two decades, 'sisterhood' characterized the principal project of the global women's movement, yet the most basic denotation of 'sisterhood' remains conflictual and inflammatory. Freighted with patriarchal familial ideology, 'sisterhood' intimates the nurturant and reproductive roles of women within that family as well as women's feelings of connection and loyalty to other women growing out of shared experiences of oppression.[1] At the same time, 'sisterhood' is aligned with the bourgeois individualism that granted 'the passage of a few middle class women into the public sphere', congealing not only *differences* in social class between them and working-class women, but crucial *differences* of social location as well. Thus 'sisterhood' evades broad-based, differentiated efforts toward the kind of social transformation that effects justice for all human persons.[2] The Aboriginal womanist theologian Anne Pattel-Gray captures the ambiguous and failed story of sisterhood across different racial, cultural, ethnic, religious, sexual, political, economic and philosophic borders when she writes, 'Not yet Tiddas.'[3] *Not yet sisters*. Thus, it is difficult and painful for diverse critical theologies committed to the radical liberation of women to speak univocally, *to speak in or under one voice*. These theologies require differentiated understandings and pluri-voiced speech. Indeed, 'difference' resists and contests any tendency toward a smothering maternalistic 'ma-'am-stream feminist theology'. Here, 'feminist' functions (as it always has in *Concilium*'s Feminist Theology series) to pluralize, to destabilize, to dismantle, to problematize any propensity to asphyxiate or suppress difference in critical theologies committed to the radical liberation of women.

I

Feminists have come to insist that the absence of considerations of difference weakens any form of feminist discourse; at the same time, this option for a pluralist rather than unitary understanding of women has fostered rich and provocative complication. Within the wide and fluid borders of critical feminist theologies, what is meant by difference? What praxial and philosophic interpretations lie behind that use? What is mediated in the analytical use of the notion of difference? What does the multiplicity invoked by difference contribute to the tasks of interdependence, collaboration and solidarity among critical feminist theologies? In so far as religious, cultural and geo-social (i.e., geo-political, -economic, and -technological) structures divide, how can and does difference empower?

Logical and epistemological difference

Several inter-related issues are posed in consideration of logical and epistemological difference. First, the use of difference in critical feminist theologies neither intends nor adverts to what deconstructionists mean by the play of *differance*. Jacques Derrida in *Of Grammatology* makes *differance* basic: it displaces, intervenes, disrupts. *Differance* resists what is invariable, yet it dissolves the tendency to absolutize dimensions of specificity or particularity in reality. Eve Sedgwick contends that the 'analytic move [deconstruction] makes is to demonstrate that categories presented in a culture as symmetrical, binary oppositions actually subsist in . . . more unsettled dynamic tacit relation'.[4] Symbiosis, affiliation and interdependence can be detected in difference. Second, behind the commonsense use of difference lie derogation and indirection; thus, any positive epistemological charge of difference may be subverted by logical opposition. Difference insinuates not merely variance, but deviation, division, discrepancy, discord, incongruity, incompatibility, inconsistency, anomaly, contrariety, aberration and misunderstanding. When such disaffirming and antagonistic intention suffuses consciousness, use of difference as a tool risks capitulation to the unitary, to the uniform, to the powerful – even to the feminist as unitary and powerful. In critical feminist theologies, the use of difference must include struggle, although not struggle for individualism or intrapsychic fulfillment or singularity or, even, separateness. Rather, difference carries forward struggle for life in its uniqueness, variation and fullness; difference is a celebrative option for life in all its integrity, in all its distinctiveness. Italian feminists apprehend this most clearly in their refusal to take equality as the conceptual opposite of difference. Rather, Italian feminists maintain that 'difference is an existential principle which concerns modes of human being, the peculiarity of one's own experiences, goals, possibilities and one's sense of existence in a given situation and in the situations one wants to create for oneself'.[5] This clarification recollects not only the colonial juridical history of the notion of equality and its invasive role in the cultures of women (and men) of the two-thirds world, but also its rigid reign over social class relations.

Third, the notion of difference in critical feminist theologies raises the problem of understanding experience. Because experience is such a general notion, speech about experience wants precision, filling out, explanation; the very generality of experience may undermine the concrete. It is preferable to speak of patterns of experience and, on this account, to distinguish several patterns – biological, psychological, dramatic, aesthetic, artistic, practical, social, intellectual, mystical. At the same time, critical feminist theologians must be wise in the apprehension and use of experience as a category of analysis. To confine difference chiefly to the world of immediacy, i.e., the world of sensible experience, is to limit experience to the 'already-out-there-now' and to condemn the human subject to the 'already-in-here-now'. On this position, what is to be known is obvious, seen and extroverted, but it can be known *really* and *only* by the subject who is having the experience. Such confinement of difference renders understanding of an 'other' and her experience impossible. Consequently, some of the deepest concerns of some critical feminist theologians are disconnected from the concerns of other and different feminist theologians. Some women protest, while other women more or less consciously acquiesce to the assertion: the experience of some particular woman or group of women cannot be understood or judged or critiqued by other and different women. An isolating relativism as well as a pernicious pluralism vitiates the ground for understanding, reflection and judgment; for evaluation, deliberation and praxis. Still, this situation presents critical feminist theologies with a distinctive epistemological challenge: to reject the ocular, totalizing, pornographic myth that knowing is taking a look, critical knowing is taking a second and good look. Critically interrogated, difference, in and of experience, prompts these theologies to probe and name experience; to understand what is common and singular and different; to question, to test insights, to judge.

Fourth, critical feminist theologies do not reject logical thinking; they use logic to debunk stereotypes; to expose ideology; to demystify systems, structures and processes that divide and oppress. These theologies take up their stand for truth at the feet of poor white, yellow, red, brown, black women. From this point of departure, critical feminist theologies insist that truth is never independent of cultural, social and historical conditions. For these theologies, the search for truth is motivated by the deepest concerns of all those who transgress the definitions of 'so-called acceptable' women – especially poor women and lesbians who embody 'indecent difference'.[6] Thus, the experience, insight, understanding and judgment of poor, oppressed and marginalized women stand as normative in any critical feminist theological formulation.

Fifth, in the search for meaning and value, critical feminist theologies interpret scriptures and scriptural traditions within different religious, historical, cultural and geo-social situations. Because these critical theologies recognize the possibility of arbitrarily cutting off questions in the search for truth, they are alert to the danger of conceding difference, while, simultaneously, levelling difference through toleration, through indifference to difference. In a critical epistemic, difference stands as 'a fund of necessary polarities between which creativity can spark like a dialectic'.[7] Thus, difference is both a source of understanding and a deterrent to the more or less conscious choice to identify and substitute partial or provisional or probable truth as truth exclusively, comprehensively.

Consider the writing of histories. Critical feminist theologies reject 'big' histories of male dominance and supremacy, meta-narratives of phallo-macho-centric conquest. These theologies affirm 'large-scale empirical narratives' that introduce local complexifying accounts which recover lost traditions and practices of female agency, creativity and resistance; narratives that reclaim female-centred practices mislabelled as natural; narratives that 'revalue previously derogated forms of women's culture'.[8] When these large-scale and local narratives engage one another dialectically, they counteract any tendencies to distort or to deceive. To give careful attention to local narratives helps to prevent large-scale ones from solidifying into 'quasi-meta-narratives'; to give careful attention to large-scale accounts helps to prevent local ones from 'devolving into *simple demonstrations of difference*'.[9]

Still, what has been said about the confrontation of critical feminist theologies with male-dominated histories must be repeated from the standpoint of women in poor, marginalized and oppressed communities. Critical feminist theologies must reject 'big' histories of female achievement and prominence. These 'gyne-centric meta-narratives' often overlook the complicity of societally privileged women in fabricating spurious identities for men of oppressed and marginalized groups: the black man as sexual beast, the red man as savage animal, the brown man as indolent, the yellow man as inscrutable. Such gyne-centric meta-narratives often ignore the complex relations of power between privileged and non-privileged women in sites of domination and oppression. Yet, precisely because they are *plural*, critical feminist theologies invite large-scale empirical narratives that will explore women's interactions across intersecting lines of difference in religion, philosophy, race, culture, ethnicity, history, geo-social situation, class and sexual orientation. These narratives are further complexified by local and particular accounts that recover, restore and revalue women's lived lives. When these large-scale and local narratives of women's lived lives engage one another dialectically, they controvert any tendency to stifle, to manipulate, to betray.

II

Difference in critical feminist perspectives does not permit some relative situation in which the privileged sit comfortably repentant beside the oppressed. Difference challenges us to overcome the societal conditioning that would have us ignore our differences or treat them with suspicion or contempt, arrogance or conceit. Difference challenges us to reject the reproduction of kyriarchal thinking. Difference instigates a new pedagogy by which to educate ourselves critically about ourselves, about 'other' and different women (and men), about our inter-relations in situations of domination and oppression. This dialectic rescinds and criss-crosses those borders or structures erected to divide, to segregate, to disempower. Such dialectical analysis not only trespasses borders but unmasks those women (and men) in whose interest and for whose material profit those perimeters have been constructed and guarded. It is in the range and seriousness of sustained plural dialectical encounters that difference gains real authority and pushes through false and pedantic antitheses as well as totalizing hegemonic world views. In this process, not only are new knowledges and resources unleashed for all women (and men), but new obligations emerge. What is at stake both for poor, oppressed and marginalized women (and their communities) and societally privileged women (and their communi-tites) is authentic praxis in the context of recognizing, grappling with, learning and celebrating difference. As Audre Lorde observes, 'In our world, divide and conquer must become define and empower.'[10]

Praxis and difference

Critical feminist theologies institute a paradigm shift in theology; integral to that shift is epistemological rupture or a new way of grasping and affirming truth. Given their critical orientation, those feminist theologies that assume the epistemological task of contesting androcentric, imperialistic and subjugating knowledges have a further challenge to social praxis. Even as praxis is a vital site of difference, difference stakes out another site for praxis.

In Christian terms, knowledge does not lead to power, but to responsibility. Since these critical theologies consciously intend what is true, what is just, they call for a social praxis that does not simply reproduce the present intellectual, cultural or geo-social situation. These theologies promote and support efforts, beginning at the feet of poor, oppressed and marginalized women, to critique, purify and transform those situations. Critical feminist theologies are wary of all forms of contrivance, of coercion, of instrumentality in the struggle for liberation. These theologies never oppose social to personal praxis; rather, personal praxis finds authentic viability in the geo-social domain. The woman (and man) active in history, in the geo-social situation, realizes herself (and himself) in new, wholesome, redemptive patterns of intersubjective communal, geo-social relation. At the same time, the woman (and the man) active in history creates new, wholesome, redemptive intersubjective, communal, geo-social relations.

Difference and moral authenticity

Since critical feminist theologies consciously intend to produce and reproduce what is true – in word and in deed – these theologies recognize an ethics of thinking, that is, truth is a way of being. It is painfully the case that the moral state of a theologian does not determine the quality of her (or his) theologizing. But critical feminist theologians acknowledge the inescapable moral relation *between* what they think and speak and write *and* the nature of the relations they form with other women (and women). For instance, most white European and North American feminists have come to understand critique as a fundamental gesture of theology. Yet, how is it that most white European and North American feminist theologians so often perceive themselves as shaping (or, at least, unconsciously assume themselves to be shaping) the theoretical script and stage for the theologizing of 'other' and different women in whose oppression they have historically participated and from which, even now, they continue to benefit? How is it possible that truly critical white European and North American feminist theologians expect their work to constitute the primary source or tradition of thought for 'other' and different women doing theology? Is it possible that truly critical white European and North American feminist theologians overlook self-criticism? Or, can truly critical womanist theologians simply impose their theological analysis as the primary source or tradition of thought for other black women doing theology in other and different geo-social situations? Is it possible that truly critical womanist theologians overlook self-criticism? Or, can truly critical minjung theologians refuse to embrace the punished and despised lesbian? Is it possible that truly critical minjung theologians overlook self-criticism? Hegemony is always a possibility, even for the oppressed. This is why we must heed Audre Lorde's caution to continual self-criticism; this is why we must be humbly, critically, attuned to our own moral and theological praxis, lest unconsciously we appropriate the attitudes, spirit, sensibility and tools of the master.[11]

Perspectival differences

Perspectival differences in critical feminist theologies can never be identified exclusively with the specificity of social location, i.e., differences in religion, culture, race, ethnicity, social class, sexual orientation. Rather, perspectives emerge from critical inquiry, understanding, reflection and judgment on social location. In so far as critical feminist theologies stress complexity, understand differences in social location and grasp their own differing formulations as provisional and probable, they *are* perspectives.

While the proper subject of critical feminist theologies is women's experiences, there can be no cheap fusion of perspectives, no indifference to the ways in which women are globally implicated, often, but not always, through no fault of their own, in the oppression of other women (and children and men). North American and European feminists must consider the impact of their daily material living on the lives of the women (and children and men) of Africa, Asia, the Caribbean, Latin America, the Pacific Basin. At the same time, socially privileged women within Africa, Asia, Latin America and the Pacific Basin must confront their co-optation in structures that oppress poor and marginalized women (and children and men) in their own geo-social situations. White European and North American women must analyse how, in their particular geo-social situations, systemic and structured racism (in its multiple forms, e.g., anti-Semitism, anti-black) erases nationality or citizenship, reducing 'other' women (and men) to simple biological physiognomy. In erasure, difference is made dangerous. European and North American women need to scrutinize, for instance, just how homophobia is sedimented in consciousness and deforms thinking. Through bias, the different are rendered a danger. At the same time, women of poor, oppressed and marginalized communities living within Europe and North America must confront their complicity in structures and institutions that assault other women (and children and men) in other oppressed and marginalized communities living in that same geo-social situation. Perhaps what is more important, women of oppressed and marginalized communities living within Europe and North America must reckon with the ways in which they have been co-opted, not only by the structures of domination, but by the destructive experience of being dominated.

III

This issue of *Concilium* explores difference as a model for understanding and expressing a new situation in theology. This chapter has interrogated some of the implications and consequences of difference in critical theologies committed to the radical liberation of women. It remains to inquire about the future of difference. What are the possibility and future of difference? What future will difference make for critical feminist theologies?

First, inasmuch as critical theologies committed to the liberation of women stem from real struggles to profess a living faith in a genuine God of hope and love, they call for deep-going conversion, not only of the theologian, but also of her cultural and social community, especially her religious community. Christian experience has long confirmed Audre Lorde's assertion that 'without community there is no liberation'.[12] But authentic community is a product neither of geography nor of the suppression of differences. Rather, authentic community emerges in the strenuous effort to understand common and different experiences; to interrogate those differences, commonalities and interdependencies rigorously; to reach common judgments; to realize and sustain interdependent commitments. As community in difference is a hard-won achievement, so too is difference in community. Such interdependence is reached only through deep-going conversion and serious, honest conversation – speaking with head and heart and flesh; listening with head and heart and flesh.

Second, when difference is grasped as 'a fund of necessary polarities', then interdependence is no longer threatening. It is important to distinguish interdependence from assimilation or absorption and loss. 'Pour your pitcher of wine into the wide river/ And where is your wine? There is only the river.'[13] How poignantly the Aboriginal poet Oodgeroo conveys the anguished ambivalence of an ancient people who, though forced to surrender much that they love, passionately defend their roots and revere their difference!

> We are different hearts and minds
> In a different body. Do not ask of us
> To be deserters, to disown our mother,
> To change the unchangeable.
> The gum cannot be changed into an oak.[14]

Assimilation disguises those latent possibilities of domination in difference that not only intimidate the formation of community with the coerced uniformity but menace the crucial role that difference plays in the self-constitution of identity.

Difference is the authentic context for interdependence. Authentic interdependent engagement of women (and men) of different histories, cultures, stories and races; of different gifts, strengths, aptitudes and skills, empowers women (and men) to envision and forge new relations, to draw new courage to decide, act and *be*. Authentic interdependent engagement of women (and men) of different religious, cultural, historical and social situations initiates new fields for differentiated social and cognitive praxis on behalf of social justice in the concrete. The interdependence of difference is a crucial condition for realizing our very full humanity.[15]

Third, solidarity is crucial to the future of difference, the future of the interdependence of difference, indeed, to the future of humanity. Unlike coalitions, those transitory aggregates that conjoin solely to manipulate advantage, rather than change or transform structures of oppression, solidarity is less self-interested and less pragmatic. Unlike partnerships, corporate relations fabricated and sustained through monetary transactions, solidarity opens us to new and creative possibilities in human relations. While much less intimate than friendship, solidarity insinuates cohesion, bonding and interdependence. In so far as solidarity is something to be achieved, it moves us on to something larger than, yet constitutive of, ourselves. Solidarity, then, is a practice. It extends the ground on which we may stand with other women (and children and men) who may be different in culture, history, religion, race, social class, sexual orientation, but without whom we have no future. Solidarity is both the result and the cause of practically intelligent collaborations that bring about new mediations and through which we are made new.

In the practice of solidarity, we recognize again the contingency of justice in our world: that is, justice is not necessary, things could be, and often are, othewise. Yet, inasmuch as critical feminist theologies are Christian, solidarity is crucial in realizing and celebrating the future of difference. Indeed, solidarity is a basic and fundamental gesture of theology. It could not be otherwise, for the incarnation is God's own radical act of solidarity, God's act of love, hope, and life enfleshed in Jesus. And is this not the task of authentic Christians of different histories, cultures, times and places – to enflesh love and hope and life wherever love and hope and life are fragile.

Notes

1. Elizabeth Fox-Genovese, 'The Personal Is Not Political Enough', *Marxist Perspectives* 2, Winter 1979–80, 94–113; see also Nancy A. Hewitt, 'Beyond the Search for Sisterhood: American Women's History in the 1980s', in *Unequal Sisters: A Multicultural Reader in US Women's History*, ed. Ellen Carol DuBois and Vicki L. Ruiz, London and New York 1990, 1–14; Bonnie Thorton Dill, '"On the Hem of Life": Race, Class, and the Prospects of Sisterhood,' in *Class, Race and Sex: The Dynamics of Control*, ed. Amy Swerdlow and Hannah Lessinger, Boston 1983, 173–88; Hester Eisenstein and Alice Jardine (ed.), *The Future of Difference*, New Brunswick 1985; Virginia Fabella, *Beyond Bonding*, Manila 1993; Chandra Talpade Mohanty, Ann Russo and Lourdes Torres (ed.), *Third World Women and the Politics of Feminism*, Bloomington and Indianapolis 1991; Stanlie M. James and Abena P. A. Busia (ed.), *Theorizing Black Feminisms: The Visionary Pragmatism of Black Women*, London and New York 1993; Gayatri Spivak, *In Other Worlds*, London and New York 1987; Iris Marion Young, *Justice and the Politics of Difference*, Princeton 1990.

2. Fox-Genovese, 'The Personal Is Not Political Enough' (n.1), 97–8.

3. Anne Pattel-Gray, 'Not yet Tiddas: An Aboriginal Womanist Critique of Australian Church Feminism', in *Freedom and Entrapment: Women Thinking Theology*, ed. Maryanne Confoy, Dorothy A. Lee and Joan Nowotny, North Blackburn 1995, 165–92.

4. Eve Kosofsky Sedgwick, *The Epistemology of the Closet*, Berkeley 1990, 9–10.

5. Paolo Bono and Sandra Kemp (ed.), 'Introduction: Coming from the South', in *Italian Feminist Thought*, Oxford 1991, 15.

6. Alessandra Bocchetti, 'The Indecent Difference', 148–61, in *Italian Feminist Thought* (n. 5); cf. Luce Irigaray, 'Sexual Difference', in Toril Moi (ed.), *French Feminist Thought: A Reader*, Oxford 1987, 118–30.

7. Audre Lorde, 'The Master's Tools Will Never Dismantle the Master's House', in *Sister Outsider*, Trumansburg 1984, 111.

8. Nancy Fraser, 'False Antitheses: A Response to Seyla Benhabib and Judith Butler', in Seyla Benhabib, Judith Butler, Drucilla Cornel, Nancy Fraser, *Feminist Contentions: A Philosophical Exchange*, New York and London 1995, 62–3.

9. Ibid., 62, emphasis mine.

10. Lorde, 'The Master's Tools Will Never Dismantle the Master's House', in *Sister Outsider* (n. 7), 112.

11. Ibid., 110–13.

12. Ibid., 112.

13. Oodgeroo, 'Assimilaton – No!', quoted in Kathie Cochrane, *Oodgeroo*, St Lucia, Queensland 1994, 74.

14. Ibid.

15. Nancy Hartsock, 'Difference and Domination in the Women's Movement: The Dialectic of Theory and Practice', in *Class, Race and Sex: The Dynamics of Control* (n. 1), 166–7.

Contributors

MARIA JOSÉ F. ROSADO NUNES is a sociologist, with a doctorate from the École des Hautes Études en Sciences Sociales in Paris. She has worked with and studied base communities in various parts of Brazil, and is currently studying Catholic thinking on abortion. She is vice president of ISER (Institute for Religious Studies) in Rio de Janeiro and a member of the Brazilian Commission on Citizenship and Reproduction, as well as lecturing on the sociology of religion in São Paulo and holding the chair of feminist studies in São Bernardo do Campo. Besides numerous articles, she has written *Vida Religiosa nos Meios Populares* (Petrópolis).

ELAINE WAINWRIGHT is an Australian of Anglo-Irish origin. She obtained her undergraduate and doctoral degrees from the University of Queensland and a Master of Arts in Theology from Catholic Theological Union in Chicago. She is currently lecturer in Biblical Studies and Feminist Studies in Theology in the Brisbane College of Theology. She lectures and conducts workshops both nationally and internationally in the area of feminist interpretations of scripture and has published a number of articles in this field. Her doctoral dissertation *Towards a Feminist Critical Reading of the Gospel according to Matthew* has been published in the series BZNW.

Address: Catholic Theological College, Approach Road, Banyo Q. 4014, Australia.

TERESIA MBARI HINGA studied at Nairobi University, and was awarded a doctorate in religious studies from the University of Lancaster, where she was the recipient of a Commonwealth Scholarship. She has taught and lectured at Kenyatta University, Harvard University and the Iliff School of Theology. Currently she is an assistant professor at De Paul University in Chicago, Illinois and is the author of several articles on the inculturation of Christianity in African contexts and the impact of colonialism on African women. She is a member of the advisory board of *The Edinburgh Review of Theology and Religion*, a member of the Ecumenical Association of Third World Theologians (EATWOT), member of the Executive Board of the African Association for the Study of Religion (AASR), and a member of the Circle of Concerned African Women Theologians.

Address: Kenyatta University, Department of Religious Studies, PO Box 43844, Nairobi, Kenya, Africa.

MONIKA JAKOBS was born in 1959 and studied Catholic theology, German and sociology in Saarbrücken and Cardiff. She has worked as a teacher in various forms of church school and in the Catholic Academy. In 1993 she gained her doctorate with a work on the question of God in feminist theology and since then has lectured on religious education in the University of Koblenz-Landau. Between 1991 and 1993 she was secretary of the European Association for Women's Theological Research.

Address: Gaulgasse 5, 76877 Offenbach a.d. Queich, Germany.

MARY E. HUNT is a feminist theologian from the Roman Catholic tradition. She is the co-founder and co-director of the Women's Alliance for Theology, Ethics and Ritual, an educational organization in Silver Spring, Maryland, USA. She currently teaches at Georgetown University. She is the author of *Fierce Tenderness: A Feminist Theology of Friendship*, and the editor of *From Woman-Pain to Woman-Vision*.

Address: WATER, Women's Alliance for Theology, Ethics and Ritual, 8035 13th Street, Suite 3, Silver Spring, Maryland 20190, USA.

GHAZALA ANWAR, born and raised in Pakistan, lives in exile in the United States where she studied religion at the University of Chicago and Temple University. She has taught Islamic studies at Colorado College, Temple University, Franklin and Marshall College, and currently teaches at Colgate University. Her method in Islamic studies is hermeneutical and literary, exploring the ways in which classical Islamic texts impinge upon contemporary Muslim life. She is a member of the Steering Committee for the Women and Religion Program Section of the American Academy of Religion (AAR).

Address: Colgate University, Department of Philosophy and Religion, Hamilton, New York 13346, USA.

CHATSUMAN KABILSINGH was born in India in 1944 and after university study in India gained her MA in Canada and her PhD in India. Since 1973 she has been teaching in the Department of Philosophy and Religion of

Thammasat University, Bangkok. She has written more than thirty books and translated important Buddhist Sutras; her specialist interest is women in Buddhism. She is President of International Buddhist Women and editor of the newsletter on Buddhist women's activities.

Address: Faculty of Liberal Arts, Thammasat University, Ta-Prachan, Bangkok 10200, Thailand.

ADELE REINHARTZ is Associate Professor in the area of Judaism and Christianity in the Greco-Roman Era, in the Department of Religious Studies, McMaster University, Hamilton, Ontario, Canada. Her main areas of research are the Fourth Gospel and literary criticism of biblical narrative. Publications include a monograph entitled *The Word in the World: The Cosmological Tale in the Fourth Gospel*, Atlanta 1982, and the commentary on the Gospel of John in *Searching the Scriptures, Vol. 2: A Feminist Commentary*, ed. Elisabeth Schüssler Fiorenza, New York 1994. Currently she is completing a book entitled *Why Ask My Name? Anonymity and Identity in Biblical Narrative*.

Address: Dept of Religious Studies, McMaster University, Hamilton, Ontario, Canada L8S 4K1.

ARUNA GNANADASON has been Coordinator of the Women's Programme within Unit III, Justice, Peace and Creation of the World Council of Churches since 1991. In 1982 she joined The National Council of Churches in India as Executive Secretary of the unit on women, playing an advocacy role for women and building a women's movement in the church, and helping church women relate to secular women's movements. She was involved with Vimochana, a forum for women's rights, in Bangalore, and other women's groups in Tamil Nadu, Bombay and Delhi. She is a member of the Ecumenical Association of Third World Theologians (EATWOT) and has been actively involved in its Women's Commission. She has contributed innumerable articles to Christian and secular journals, magazines and books on a wide variety of topics – especially on issues related to women and to North-South relations. She has edited several publications including the regular newsletter of the Ecumenical Decade of the Churches in Solidarity with Women – the *Decade Link*. She is the author of *No Longer A Secret: The Church and Violence Against Women* (WCC).

Address: The Women's Desk, World Council of Churches, PO Box 2100, 1211 Geneva 2, Switzerland.

JACQUELINE FIELD-BIBB holds degrees in sociology and in theology. She received a doctorate from London University in 1988 which was published under the title *Women Towards Priesthood: Ministerial Politics and Feminist Praxis* (1991). She has published various articles on the subject of women and ministry and on aspects of feminist theology.

Address: 33 Arlow Road, London N21 3JS, England.

DAVID TRACY was born in 1939 in Yonkers, New York. He is a priest of the diocese of Bridgeport, Connecticut, and a doctor of theology of the Gregorian University, Rome. He is The Greeley Distinguished Service Professor of Philosophical Theology at the Divinity School of Chicago University. He is the author of *The Achievement of Bernard Lonergan* (1970), *Blessed Rage for Order: New Pluralism in Theology* (1975), *The Analogical Imagination* (1980), and *Plurality and Ambiguity* (1987).

Address: University of Chicago, Divinity School/Swift Hall, 1025 East 58th Street, Chicago, Ill. 60637, USA.

MARCIANO VIDAL was born in the Province of León in Spain on 14 June 1937. He is a Redemptorist priest and lectures in moral theology at the Comillas University in Madrid and the Higher Institute of Moral Sciences, of which he is currently Director. His works include *Moral del amor y de la sexualidad* (1971, trans. into Italian and Portuguese), *Moral de Actitudes* (3 vols., 1974–81, trans. into Italian and Portuguese), *El dicernimiento ético* (1980), *Moral del matrimonio* (1980), *La educación moral en la escuela* (1981) and *La moral laica en la sociedad secular* (1983).

NORBERT METTE was born in Barkhausen/porta, Germany in 1946. After studying theology and sociology he gained a doctorate in theology, and since 1984 he has been Professor of Practical Theology at the University of Paderborn. He is married with three children, and is an Editorial Director of *Concilium*. He has written numerous works on pastoral theology and religious education, including: *Voraussetzungen christlicher Elementarerziehung*, Düsseldorf 1983; *Kirche auf dem Weg ins Jahr 2000* (with M. Blasberg-Kuhnke), Düsseldorf 1986; *Gemeindepraxis in Grundbegriffen* (with C. Bäumler), Munich and Düsseldorf 1987; *Auf der Seite der Unterdrückten? Theologie der Befreiung im Kontext Europas* (ed. with P. Eicher), Düsseldorf 1989; *Der Pastorale Notstand* (with O. Fuchs), Düsseldorf 1992.

Address: Liebigweg 11a, D 48165 Münster, Germany.

JULIA CHING was born 1933 in Shanghai, China. She studied in Asia, the United States and Europe, and received her doctorate from the Australian National University in Canberra, where she was also a lecturer in Asian civilizations. She later taught at Columbia University and at Yale University. She is also an associate member of the Institute of Oriental Religions of Sophia University in Tokyo and is at present professor of religious studies at the University of Toronto. She has published in many professional journals, and her books include *To Acquire Wisdom: The Way of Wang Yang-ming*, New York 1976, a study of the fifteenth-century Chinese philosopher, and *Confucianism and Christianity. A Comparative Study*, Tokyo and New York 1977.

Address: Victoria College, University of Toronto, 73 Queen's Park Crescent, Toronto, Ontario M5S 1K7, Canada.

WILLIAM R. BURROWS, managing editor of Orbis Books, Maryknoll, New York, has worked as a missionary in Papua New Guinea and as an inner city pastor in African American Catholic parishes in the United States. He holds a doctorate in theology from the University of Chicago, is author of *New Ministries: The Global Context*, and is working on a book on mission and inter-religious relations in a postmodern world.

Address: PO Box 308, Maryknoll, New York 10545–0308, USA.

GABRIELE DIETRICH is professor at the Tamilnadu Theological Seminary, Madurai, in the Department of Social Analysis, and also teaches feminist theology. She is a well-known activist in the women's movement, and at present state vice-president of Pennurimai Iyakkam (Movement for Women's Rights) which consists of women in the informal sector. Originally from Berlin, Germany, she has lived and worked in India for twenty-four years and has become an Indian citizen.

Address: Tamilnadu Theological Seminary, Arasaradi, Madurai 625010, India.

REBECCA CHOPP teaches at the University of Chicago Divinity School. She received a PhD from the University of Chicago in 1983, and her master's degree from Saint Paul School of Theology in 1977. She works in the area of contemporary theology with a special emphasis in new forms of systematic thought.

Address: University of Chicago, The Divinity School, 1025 East 58th Street, Chicago, Ill. 60637, USA.

ELIZABETH GREEN was born in England, but now lives and works in southern Italy. A Baptist pastor, she gained her doctorate in theology at the Pontifical University of Salamanca, Spain. She has taught feminist theology at the Baptist faculty of Rüschlikon, Switzerland and the Waldensian Faculty in Rome. As well as articles she has written *Dal silenzio alla parola. Storie di donne nella Bibbia*, Turin 1992, and is working on a book on the pastoral ministry of women in the Protestant churches in Italy.

Address: Cso Sonnino 23, 70121 Bari, Italy.

MARCELLA ALTHAUS-REID is an Argentinian Quaker feminist theologian. She is director of a MTh course in Theology and Development and a lecturer in Christian Ethics and Practical Theology in the University of Edinburgh, Scotland. She obtained her Bachelor in Theology from ISEDET, Buenos Aires, and her PhD on the influence of Paul Ricoeur on the hermeneutical circle of Liberation Theology from St Andrews University, Scotland. Prior to studying for her doctorate she was co-ordinator of a conscientization process in deprived areas of Dundee and Perth. She is a member of the Asociacion de Teologas y Pastoras de Latinoamerica y del Caribe and the Association of European Women in Theological Research. Her publications include *Walking with Women Serpents* (1993), *When God is a White, Rich Woman who Does Not Walk* (1994), and *Doing Murguera Theology in Britain* (1995). Her work in progress includes a book on mariology, two books on Latin American feminist theology (as editor), and several contributions to collections of essays on popular hermeneutics.

Address: 5 Grange Terrace, Edinburgh EH9 2LD, Scotland.

M. SHAWN COPELAND is associate professor of theology (systematics) at Marquette University in Milwaukee, Wisconsin. She received her doctoral degree from Boston College. The author of more than thirty book chapters, articles, reviews and commentary in professional journals, she co-edits with Professor Elisabeth Schüssler Fiorenza the Feminist Theology section of *Concilium*. She co-chairs with Joan M. Martin the Program Section on Women and Religion of the American Academy of Religion (AAR), is a member of the Board of Directors of the Catholic Theological Society of America (CTSA), and Associate Convenor of the Black Catholic Theological Symposium. Her present research interests focus on solidarity and suffering in critical feminist theologies and the contributions of African American women to African American critical thought.

Address: Marquette University, Department of Theology, Milwaukee, Wisconsin 53233, USA.

Members of the Advisory Committee for Feminist Theology

Directors

Mary Shawn Copeland	New Haven, Conn	USA
Elisabeth Schüssler Fiorenza	Cambridge, Mass	USA

Members

Marcella Althaus-Reid	Edinburgh	Scotland
Maria Pilar Aquino	San Diego	USA
Anne Carr	Chicago	USA
Mary Collins OSB	Washington, DC	USA
Denise Couture	Montreal	Canada
Wandea Deifelt	Sao Leopoldo RS	Brazil
Gabrielle Dietrich	Madurai	India
Monique Dumais	Rimouski, Quebec	Canada
Felisa Elizondo Aragón	Madrid	Spain
Irmtraud Fisher	Graz	Austria
Ivone Gebara	Recife	Brazil
Elizabeth Green	Gravina in Puglia	Italy
Mary Grey	Southampton	England
Theresia Hinga	Nairobi	Kenya
Mary Hunt	Silver Spring, Maryland	USA
Anne Jensen	Tübingen	Germany
Turid Karlsen-Seim	Oslo	Norway
Marianne Katoppo	Jakarta Selatan	Indonesia
Ursula King	Bristol	England
Mary-John Mananzan	Manila	Philippines
Silvia Marcos	Cuernavaca	Mexico
Hedwig Meyer-Wilmes	Nijmegen	Netherlands
Christine Schaumberger	Kassel	Germany
Donna Singles	Lyons	France
Regula Strobel	Freiburg	Switzerland
Lieve Troch	Breda	Netherlands
Elaine Wainwright	Benyo	Australia

Members of the Board of Directors

Some Back Issues of *Concilium* still available

All listed issues published before 1991 are available at £6.95 each. Issues published after 1991 are £8.95 each. Add 10% of value for postage.
US, Canadian and Philippian subscribers contact: Orbis Books, Shipping Dept., Maryknoll, NY 10545 USA

Special rates are sometimes available for large orders. Please write for details.

1990

1991

1992

1993

1994

Please send orders and remittances to:
SCM Press Ltd, 26-30 Tottenham Road, London N1 4BZ

Concilium Subscription Information
- outside North America

Individual Annual Subscription (1996 six issues): £30.00

Institution Annual Subscription (1996 six issues): £40.00

Airmail subscriptions: add £10.00

Individual issues: £8.95 each

New subscribers please return this form:
for a two-year subscription, double the appropriate rate

1996 *Concilium* subscriptions   ☐ £30.00   ....
(for individuals)

1996 *Concilium* subscriptions   ☐ £40.00   ....
(for institutions)

For airmail postage outside Europe   ☐ + £10.00   ....
(optional) please add £10.00

Total . . . .

I wish to subscribe for one/two years as an individual/institution
(delete as appropriate)

Name . . . .

Address . . . .

. . . .

. . . . Postcode . . . .

I enclose a cheque for . . . . made payable to SCM Press Ltd

Please charge my Access/Visa/Mastercard No ..../............/............/...........

Signature....................................... Expiry Date...................................

Please send this form to:
**SCM Press Ltd (Concilium) 9-17 St Albans Place London N1 0NX
Credit card telephone orders on: 0171-359 8033   Fax: 0171-359 0049**